DATE DUE

BEYOND DANCE

BEYOND DANCE

Laban's Legacy of Movement Analysis

EDEN DAVIES

Illustrations by Steve Hurst

Routledge
Taylor & Francis Group
New York   London

Published in 2006 by
Routledge
Taylor & Francis Group
711 Third Avenue
New York, NY 10017

Published in Great Britain by
Routledge
Taylor & Francis Group
2 Park Square
Milton Park, Abingdon
Oxon OX14 4RN

International Standard Book Number-10: 0-415-97728-2 (Softcover) 0-415-97727-4 (hardcover)
International Standard Book Number-13: 978-0-415-97728-9 (Softcover) 978-0-415-97728-9 (hardcover)

Library of Congress Cataloging-in-Publication Data

Catalog record is available from the Library of Congress

Taylor & Francis Group
is the Academic Division of Informa plc.

Visit the Taylor & Francis Web site at
http://www.taylorandfrancis.com

and the Routledge Web site at
http://www.routledge-ny.com

CONTENTS

ILLUSTRATIONS

ACKNOWLEDGMENTS

The majority of the information in this book is from my memory of the times I have worked with Warren Lamb, first in the 1960s and more recently in the 1990s. This is reinforced by the access given to me to his personal papers, and extensive discussions with him in recent months. Without his encouragement and consistent support this book would not have been possible, and for this I am deeply grateful.

I was also given full cooperation and help at the two archives I used, that at the National Resource Centre for Dance at the University of Surrey, and also at High House, Dartington Hall, and to the archivists there I also extend my thanks.

Many other people have helped with specific information and among them I mention Dr Carol-Lynne Moore at the University of Surrey School of Performing Arts; Anita Hall, President of Action Profiling International and Bunny Martin, Director of the Body Action Campaign. In particular I would like to thank playwright Ronald Harwood for his very valuable advice.

It is exciting to use the Andy Warhol sketches and a great deal of energy went into trying to trace them after all these years. Richard Philp, Executive Director of *Dance Magazine*, and Marjorie King at the Andy Warhol Museum in Pittsburg both were generous with their time in helping Warren Lamb and myself. I hope they enjoyed the pursuit as much as we did.

Of the companies mentioned I approached two for help and I am grateful that this was immediately forthcoming. These were Mrs Kay Nichols and Ms Julie Harford at Mars® (MI & R Winnersh) and Mr P.R. Warr, Group Managing Director of Faithful Group Ltd.

Lastly it has been a great pleasure to work again with artist and sculptor Steve Hurst who supplied the drawings.

FOREWORD

Eden Davies tells a good story. It starts with Rudolf Laban, a genius who died in 1958 and is only now beginning to be recognized for the full scope and significance of his ideas. He was an extraordinarily creative thinker who influenced many of the leading European intellects of the first half of the twentieth century.

Laban is still primarily known for his career in the world of Dance. Yet he himself was always looking beyond "Dance" in the colloquial sense of the term, whether ballet, folk or ballroom, to the significance of the harmonies and rhythms of how people move in their everyday lives. It is in this respect that his influence has been more significant, and can become even more so if it is not confined within the strict conventional category of "Dance".

The story continues with focus on my research and how it was applied and developed. The author gives a clear explanation of theory and builds it into her description of events so as to have the potential of achieving a goal for which many have strived in vain – a book about Movement Analysis which can be easily understood by anyone who moves i.e. everyone. Part of the ease of understanding is the flow of the writing itself.

Eden Davies is well qualified to take on this venture. She worked in my organization for some years and has remained more or less in touch, but chose to remain an observer of developments rather than become a professional practitioner. Had a writer been looking around for a subject out of which to create a book he or she may well have chosen some aspect of "Body Movement". The spate of books on "Body Language" has come and gone leaving a conversational term which everyone uses, but they mostly do so inaccurately, superficially, and devoid of context. There is a case for the study of body movement to be offered as much more substantiated and the author makes it eloquently. She is able to do so because she is obviously a penetrating observer with a keen kinaesthetic sense and has maintained continuity in practising these faculties.

Her concern that the recognition of Laban's concepts "Beyond Dance" may become lost is addressed in the book and she may well help to open up a new field of study. Currently "Movement Study" exists at university level almost exclusively as an adjunct of Dance Departments. Interest is beginning to be aroused in other fields, however, such as anthropology and electronics, and it needs to be catered for.

As the story develops Eden Davies incorporates more of her own research and opinions, and this enhances the interest. Her writing on the gender implications, for example, is both prescient and stimulating as well as topical.

To date most entrants into the field of professional Movement Analysis have been ex-dancers looking for a new career. The trickle of people with a non-dance background could become a flood once the potential is realized. The story told in this book could revolutionize how people become aware of the extent to which they "dance" in their own lives and its significance beyond the theatre, discotheque or ballroom.

Warren Lamb
Los Angeles
February 2001

INTRODUCTION

In 1938 a Hungarian-born choreographer called Rudolf Laban arrived in Britain. For thirty years he had been one of the major figures on the European dance scene, and more than any other single person was responsible for shaping the modern Central European dance movement. Under his influence dance had been placed on an equal footing with the other arts. It had also been placed in a wider context as an activity for the whole community, reflecting his deep philosophical interest in the potential of the human body and spirit. Dance, he believed, should grow naturally out of the rhythm inherent in every individual, a rhythm which should find expression in their everyday life. In all this he reflected the intellectual concern of the time, expressed by artists from every discipline, with man's relationship to increasing mechanization and urbanization. The human spirit had to be elevated and an outlet for this was the Folk Movement. Laban led the way with contemporary folk dances and massive dance choirs for which he was particularly famous, and the new folk dances drew their inspiration from the modern industrial environment.

The England Laban arrived in had generally little time for such ideas; dance was regarded as an activity unrelated to any other type of movement, belonging either on the stage or in the ballroom. But the intellectual movements on the continent had not entirely passed England by and he found enough fertile ground, particularly among educationalists, many of whom had already travelled to study in his schools or those of his pupils during the 20s and 30s.

Laban's contribution to dance, choreography, and especially to dance in education, was enormously significant but very little of it survives today in its original form. As it happens it was only part of his legacy. To Laban dance was the supreme expression of the human condition. But the most menial task in the operation of a machine held for him just as much importance and potential beauty in the effort and shaping of the body required to perform it. It was part of the total human dance. To neglect the importance of such ordinary movement would, he believed, make men increasingly like machines themselves with dysfunctional lives. It was this study of the rhythmic movement of people at work, begun in Germany, which was to lead to his most original work in Britain, and its development was only possible because of his best known invention and lasting legacy – Labanotation.

How his methods for observing and notating movement devolved is a story of the pursuit of an abstract ideal in the face of sometimes insuperable odds. It is a story which owes as much to his many disciples as it does to the charismatic Laban himself. The reputation of Labanotation is alive and well. Many institutions throughout the world bear his name and use his notation, mostly to record dance or for dance therapy, and most of these have combined it with some other discipline or theory.

Less commonly known is how Labanotation opened the way for a deeper and more scientific analysis of what constitutes human movement. From its roots in recording choreography so that a dance score could be handed on as accurately as a piece of music, it was adapted when he came to Britain to record human movement at work. Operative tasks in agriculture and in industry were set down not just as a record but in order to find the most efficient way of performing a task. To do this necessitated knowing not simply what movements were made, but what qualities the movement contained in terms of space, time and pressure. These Effort notations were developed and put alongside the original Labanotation making it possible to record the most minute aspects of movement. The result was to demonstrate that no two people perform the same task in quite the same way. The remarkable development of this, and the main subject of this book, was the discovery that how a person performs one task reflects the way in which they will deal with any task or any problem, mental or practical.

In other words, we each have a movement pattern which we carry around with us. It is totally individual and we use it in everything we do; to be prevented from using it for long periods will put us under stress. This movement pattern can be detected by a trained observer in the course of a normal interview and the topic discussed in the interview is of absolutely no consequence. Analysis of our movement pattern reveals not only how we will perform in work situations, but also a great deal about our personality and our capacity for personal relationships.

This analysis of individual aptitudes and personality through movement observation inspired by Laban is potentially the most important part of his legacy and it also remains largely true to his original work. Sadly, in its purest form it is in the hands of relatively few practitioners and applied largely in executive selection. But many hundreds of people from a variety of walks of life have, over the years, received basic training in movement analysis, and have gone on to incorporate its basic principles into their existing methods of therapy or analysis. Recent trainees in Britain are transactional therapists. Warren Lamb worked with Laban in the final years of his life and the secrets of this method of analysis have until recently rested largely with him. He has been almost solely responsible for carrying forward Laban's discovery about the nature of human movement. It is to be hoped that now the survival of this very specific and valuable body of knowledge is not entirely dependent on him.

A further danger has always been the natural attraction of such a subject to off-beat cults. On the one hand there are those with a penchant for sensationalising personality analysis, and on the other there are those attracted by its commercial potential. Neither feels any overwhelming allegiance to the origins of movement observation in Laban's philosophy. Used correctly movement observation is a skilled and totally objective method of determining individual potential. Several times during recent decades Warren Lamb has had to take a stand to protect his work from plagiarisation by people happy to ignore its roots. For this reason more than any other it is important that the story is at last told so that there can never be any doubt about the origins and basis of analysis through movement observation and notation.

It is a subject at once both simple and complex. Each step on the way to the complete picture is essential to the understanding of the next. These 'building blocks' are in themselves pure common-sense, but they have to be painstakingly fitted together logically for the final picture to be understood.

Laban in 1950

CHAPTER ONE

LABAN IN EUROPE

HIS EARLY LIFE

Rudolph Jean Marie Attila Laban was born in Bratislava, Hungary on December 12, 1879 to parents of French descent. His life and education were cosmopolitan. He travelled extensively in the Austro-Hungarian Empire with his military father and was for a while a cadet himself, before throwing this up for artistic studies. It was a time of tremendous intellectual change and excitement, both in Paris where he lived on-and-off from 1900 to 1907, as well as in the Schwabing bohemian district of Munich where he lived at various times as a young man. Throughout his early years he was at the heart of and involved in the foremost intellectual fashions of the time. In Paris he studied painting and architecture, and made his living as a poster artist. His interest was mostly in drawing the human form, in particular in caricaturing it and the salon society he encountered in Paris. From his youth he had a fascination with the theatre, discouraged by his parents, but his artistic skills soon led him into stage design, and from that into a deeper involvement in theatrical life.

It was also in Paris that he first met leading dance personalities such as Dalcroze, Delsarte and Isadora Duncan. Although he claimed not to accept their attitudes to dance, it seems inevitable that the dialogue they set up must have influenced Laban in formulating his ideas. This is particularly the case with Dalcroze, who shared Laban's interest in festivals and his belief that the rediscovery of rhythm through community dancing would regenerate man as a social being.

Laban absorbed and was part of the many rich intellectual movements he encountered. In Vienna where he lived as a child and adolescent, psychology and psychoanalysis were the new learning; concern was with the nature of the psyche and the soul, with discovering the power of sex and eroticism. In Paris he encountered and was deeply involved with the esoteric Rosicrucian religion, the impact of which on his philosophy can hardly be over-emphasized. Myth and legend which were important to them feature largely in his choreography. Their belief in the cosmic quality of man and his close relationship with nature were equally important to his philosophy, and their Platonic concepts of the geometry of the universe also find a direct reflection in his view of man's use of space. Their search for fundamental truth, simplicity and harmony, their claim to mystic wisdom, the pursuit of the ideal in all art forms, all became part of his philosophical basis for movement study.

Concern was with basic form. In abstract art, colour itself was seen to have form. The medium was the message. Thinking had to be liberated from restriction, the essence of truth was the goal. Just as Schoenberg liberated music from the traditional harmonic values, so Laban saw that movement should itself be liberated from music and set steps. The commitment had to come from the dancer; the inner attitude of the person moving would give movement its dynamism. Only when this had been achieved could sound be put back into movement to enhance its expression. Fashion in all disciplines was away from impressionism and into expressionism. As long as dance was an impression or interpretation of the music, it could not be an expression in its own right.

As a teenager Laban stood in the wings of a theatre and watched a series of tableaux depicting the changes of the seasons. Between each the curtain was dropped while the actors arranged themselves for the next tableau. He thought how much better it would be if the curtain stayed up and the audience could watch the actors resolve one tableau into the other with a fanfare of music. He was allowed to try out his idea and discovered he had created a dance. It was greeted with tumultuous applause. By 1913 Laban was putting poster painting behind him and concentrating on choreography and dance, although he never entirely separated himself from the visual arts and architecture. As he became a leading figure on the dance scene in Germany, he was able to put into practice the theories he had developed from the intellectual climate in which he had grown up. But it was by no means an easy ride.

The death in Paris of his wife after the birth of their second child drove him into depression and he returned for a while to Vienna. The death of his father shortly after that left him without an allowance and his mother on a small pension. Illness, depression and poverty were to dog him throughout his life, but neither these nor the permanent chaos of his domestic life ever deterred him from pursuing his vision. By 1911 he had moved to Munich, married a singer, Maja Lederer, and found work with the carnival season there, arranging lavish parties and costume entertainments. His domestic arrangements were consistently unorthodox and impecunious but Maja remained devoted to him for the rest of her life. It was this total disregard for the mundane, and the selfless devotion of the many women in his life to his sense of mission which allowed him to achieve formidable amounts.

He paid a price with his health, however, and periods of intense work were constantly followed by months of illness and depression.

A recent movement analysis of Laban by Warren Lamb (see Appendix I) puts forward a theory to explain the recurring cycle of intense creative activity followed by bouts of illness. It was, he suggests, the result of Laban's capacity for phenomenal amounts of innovative creativity, without a complementary ability to tolerate organization. When things required control and discipline it all became too much for him and he retreated into ill health. His charisma ensured there was always someone there to pick up the pieces.

In one such period of sickness he went to Dresden to take a cure, there renewing his acquaintance with Suzanne Perrottet, one of Dalcroze's leading pupils, with whom he formed a close relationship. Together they explored a world of dance where music was not the determinant of rhythm. His reputation as a movement specialist and as a movement director grew rapidly but was never profitable. Intensive teaching had to be supported by frenetic work on the winter carnivals, arranging functions that frequently required his attention all night.

ASCONA AND AFTER

In Ascona in the Swiss canton of Ticino, an experimental centre for living had been created by fashionable Bohemians who aimed to find release for man from the burden of bourgeois urban life. Laban and his entourage, then living in Munich, were naturally attracted to it, and moved there for the summer of 1913. Here Perrottet was music teacher and Maja his wife was in charge of singing, and other jobs were given to whoever turned up. One who arrived as a pupil with huge talent was Mary Wigman, and like so many more, she fell in love with Laban. According to Valerie Preston Dunlop, a later student of Laban's and his most recent biographer, Wigman, unlike most other female pupils, was rejected sexually by Laban. Valerie Preston Dunlop suggests this was to be the spur to her rivalling him as a dance teacher with a lasting impact on German dance.

The group in Ascona grew their own vegetables, cooked their own food, wove their own cloth, and danced on the open hillside barefoot and sometimes nude in celebration of life and nature. In the fashionable Avant Garde cult of idealism, the proper place to pursue beauty was through nature rather than in the restrictive environment of a theatre. When Laban later produced designs for a theatre it was with a domed roof perhaps to mimic the Ascona skies.

By the end of the season Laban's reputation as a teacher of dance was firmly established, and the direction of his work had become clear. He had developed his 'scales' of movement, rather like scales of music, which were to remain basic to his movement training. Known as the Schwungskalen (swinging scales) these were large movements involving the whole body, where the second swing grew out of the first as it returned to its beginning. The movements he claimed arose naturally out of human behaviour, all of which operated along certain planes with their ultimate reach defining the limit of our Kinesphere – 'the bubble' in which we all move. His five-point, six-point and eight-point scales from then on were daily warm-up exercises used by his students.

Returning to Munich, the group opened their first school for Tanz, Ton, Wort (The School of Art for Dance, Sound and Word), at which Mary Wigman was a pupil. After a successful winter they returned to Ascona in summer 1914, only to have the season cut short by the outbreak of war. When the students and performers fled, Laban and his female entourage were left on the hillside.

For Laban the years of the First World War were intensely difficult domestically, but at the same time proved some of the most formative philosophically. On the one hand there was the problem of housing and feeding not only Maja, Suzanne and their three children, but also his mother and younger sister who, due to the war, had lost access to their military pension. He managed to find a studio for himself in Zurich and, through a devoted woman student, accommodation in a farmhouse 30 kilometres away. The liberal lifestyle of their menage did nothing to endear them to the rural Swiss, especially with both Maja and Suzanne pregnant, and Laban was constantly beset with problems of finance, health and nationality, so these were far from happy times.

But Zurich attracted many intellectuals, among them the Dadaists, Isadora Duncan and most significantly for Laban, Carl Gustav Jung. Jung's theory of the basic antitheses in the human psyche between intuition and sensing, thinking and feeling, had for Laban a resonance with his own emerging notions of movement which he saw as consisting of time, space, weight and flow. He was also in sympathy with Jung's ideas on Racial and Universal Unconscious, and the importance in society of primitive ritual and myth.

In August 1917 the whole Laban party returned to Ascona, as part it seems of a fringe masonic lodge which Laban had joined, which allowed the participation of women. Here for audiences seated on the hillside, they performed dances to the sun and moon. There was the daytime *Song to the Sun*, the evening *Song to the Setting Sun*, a midnight dance *Demons of the Night*, and at dawn *The Rising Sun*.

Laban then succumbed to the influenza epidemic which swept across Europe in 1918 killing more people than the Great War. The cost of his lengthy treatment led to his most impecunious period, even to sleeping in the waiting-room of Nuremburg station. Nationality also remained a problem, as Bratislava where he had been born was now in Czechoslovakia instead of Hungary. The struggle to attain German citizenship, which in itself would later become a problem, now preoccupied him.

His companion at this time was the Russian dancer Dussia Bereska, with whom he set up house eventually in Stuttgart, and who bore him a son. Suzanne Perottet and Maja, each with his children remained devoted but lived elsewhere. According to Valerie Preston Dunlop, Maja actually divorced Laban in 1926 but he chose not to tell anyone, as Maja remained as loyal as ever. Throughout his later life he was able to use the excuse that he was still married as a reason for not marrying any of his subsequent partners.

Laban's name and influence now spread rapidly. Movement choirs and schools appeared in his name in several German towns. The eventual publication in 1920 of *Die Welt des Tanzers* put him firmly in the forefront of modern dance. More than that it drew attention to the importance of dance which he believed was in danger of being treated as a poor relation to other arts. Mary Wigman was gradually making her own name with a successful school, and this in itself was an advertisement for Laban, though they would later become rivals.

In 1926 during a performance of *Don Juan* in Nuremberg, Laban leapt off the stage, but the mattresses where he was to land had not been put in place. He suffered concussion and back injury and never performed as a dancer again. He continued to tour energetically nonetheless, and was briefly in the United States. Apart from American Indian dance, that visit left him unimpressed apparently and he never returned.

Great as Laban's name became in choreography and dance, and he was certainly the major player on this scene, remarkably little of that is left on paper today. His lasting contribution has been the philosophy and theory he brought to the study of movement, and in particular his achievement in recording movement. He was aware that a reason for dance having a lower profile than other arts was quite simply the limited way in which it could be handed on from one generation to another, from one country to another. The pursuit of a comprehensive script for recording all aspects of movement in terms of space, weight and time as well as body movement, became of paramount importance to him.

LABANOTATION

Systems of notation of dance existed for many centuries, possibly even in Egyptian, Greek and Roman times, and certainly in the Middle Ages. The earliest known manuscripts are in Spain and date from the 15th Century. Progress generally was slow, however, and sporadic experimentation with various systems usually led nowhere. As Ann Hutchinson points out in Labanotation, the most authoritative work on Laban's system:

"It is significant that music notation, which opened the way for the development in the art of music as we know it today, was first conceived in its modern form in the 11th Century, but it was not established as a uniform system till the beginning of the 18th Century. Dance notation got off to a much later start and has undergone a long succession of false attempts."

The first substantial progress came with the proliferation and interest in professional dance in Louis XIV's France when dance was a most fashionable pastime, and it was chic to be able to read dance scores. Raoul Feuillet published *Choreographie, ou l'Art de decrire la Danse* in 1700, drawing on a system already begun by Beauchamp, the most famous choreographer of the century. The system was adequate to a time when memory was a large factor in handing on dance – when it was sufficient to record only footwork. Mannered movements of head and hand and the rhythm of the steps would all be automatically known. The book satisfied the requirements of the time and was translated throughout Europe.

In the 19th Century stick figures were widely used, notably by Arthur Saint Leon and Albert Zorm, enabling the actions of other parts of the body to be simply represented. This system was actually added to sheet music by Vladimir Stepanov (in *Alphabet des Mouvements du Corps Humain* in 1892) so that rhythm could also be accurately indicated, but it was cumbersome and although extensively used for ballet for some time, eventually fell into disuse.

With the development of modern dance after the turn of the century, there was an increasing need to find a way of recording fluid movement, to allow for a third dimension. In 1928 two works simultaneously provided this. In England Margaret Morris published *Notation of Movement* describing a system based on anatomy, primarily for use in physical therapy. At the same time Rudolf Laban in Vienna produced *Schrifttanz*. In this the main innovation was the use of a vertical staff to represent time, the immediate advantage of which was that continuity of movement could be indicated. The two sides of the staff represented the right and left sides of the body and the length of each symbol showed the time taken by each part of the movement, so that timing could also be accurately represented. The simplicity and adaptability meant it could be applied to all types of movement.

Schrifttanz was the culmination of Laban's perseverance with notation from 1900 to 1928. He was by now a leading figure in the Choreographisches Institut, a body opened in 1926, shortly after his return from the United States, which drew together all aspects of the European dance scene. The Institut published its pocket-sized booklet saying what it was about, and putting dance notation firmly at the centre of the promotion of dance in the community.

In the summer of 1927 a remarkable meeting took place at a summer school in Bad Mergentheim to iron out the details of his system. Laban, as was well known, was outstanding for his original thought, but had little patience with detail and especially with anything called a 'system'. At the meeting were, among others, Laban's most eminent disciples, Leeder, Jooss, Bereska and Knust. The vertical staff allowing for continuity of movement had already been accepted and was of paramount importance to Laban. Shapes and symbols representing each part of the body, with a dot to mark the part of the body taking weight, were also already accepted. The problem was to organize all these in the most readable way. It was apparently Jooss who came up with the suggestion of opening up the matrix to have the symbols running parallel to each other along the page, on the left and right of the central staff. [Fig. 1] It meant that gestures, for example of the arm or hand, were given equal significance on paper to postural movements of the body, but Laban had to accept this compromise, and the system was immediately launched in a preliminary booklet *Tanzschreibstube* in order to copyright it. The name given to the notation was *kinetographie* to distinguish it from Feuillet's 18th Century *choreographie*. As in the earlier century, reading and writing dance notation again had its own fashionable cachet.

In 1928 Knust used kinetographie to great effect for a production of *Titan*. This was a choral work devised by Laban after his trip to the United States, and inspired by his experience there of American Indian dance. In *A Life for Dance* he described it as "a dance-play telling of the strength of the common hope which lies in a common will to achieve something better". Employing both soloists and dance choirs it was the perfect vehicle for the new system, which was further under-pinned by the work of the Choreographisches Institut.

The history of notation did not end there, either for Labanotation as it later became known, or for other methods. Modern technology has inspired new ideas such as those of Noel Ashkol and Abraham Wachmann, and the *choreology* of Joan and Rudolph Benesh. Labanotation has been the most enduring and most

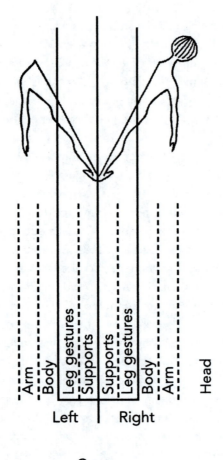

Arm
Body
Leg gestures
Supports
Supports
Leg gestures
Body
Arm
Head

Left | Right

Center
Line

Fig. 1. The opening up of the central staff to indicate movement of different parts of the body. This matrix would be further extended when necessary for more detailed recording, for example the handling of props. (Reproduced with kind permission from *Labanotation* by Ann Hutchinson, Oxford University Press, 1970.)

generally used however. It has been preserved and developed by the Dance Notation Bureau in New York, a non-profit-making organization founded in 1940 as a clearing-house for ideas on notation. The Bureau has successfully worked to get uniformity in usage and practice, to the extent that dance notation is arguably now more accurate than music notation.

While the originator of Labanotation is quite clearly Laban, it is typical of him that it was left to his disciples to refine and polish it. He was always opposed to too much systematization himself, and consequently left room for those he inspired to work within the parameters he set. Albercht Knust and later Ann Hutchinson carried out this work in Labanotation, just as Warren Lamb did for Effort and Shape writing. Laban was not always cooperative when he thought his work was being systematized however. Warren Lamb recalls a day when Laban received a letter from Ann Hutchinson asking how a particular movement should be recorded. She suggested two possibilities, stated her preference, and said that she would use this one if she did not hear from Laban within a few weeks. Laban reacted furiously at being given an ultimatum. "She doesn't understand," he roared, "She cannot do that."

In *Labanotation* Ann Hutchinson describes the three areas to be covered by notation:

1. Motif Writing – the general statement – the Nouns
2. Effort-Shape – the description – the Adjectives
3. Structural – the description of space/time/dynamics – the Adverbs

For Motif Writing which is the initial concern here, the central staff indicates the existence and duration of a movement and a double line across the staff at the beginning and end marks the start and finish of each phrase of movement. The page could therefore be laid on the floor or on a table horizontally in front of the reader, and it would be clear which represented the right or left side of the dancer. Columns on each side of the staff then show the simultaneous movement of each part of the body. The shape of the unit of movement indicated direction [Fig. 2], and further signs depicted specific parts of the body [Fig. 3]. Regular lines across the staff would show timing or rhythm [Fig. 4].

Kinetography not only marked the breakthrough necessary for the choreographer recording modern dance, but was also adaptable for use in Laban's early work in industry, dealing as it did with every aspect of body movement. It was more than a simple guide through set movements such as Feuillet's system which assumed a general knowledge of rhythm and gestures. In addition to giving directions for movement, Kinetography could also record how a position was arrived at by one individual compared with another. With the later addition of Effort and Shape notation, the most minute degree of movement could be recorded for objective study. Crucially, the adaptability of Kinetography to non-performance movement opened up a vista of possibilities.

DIRECTION

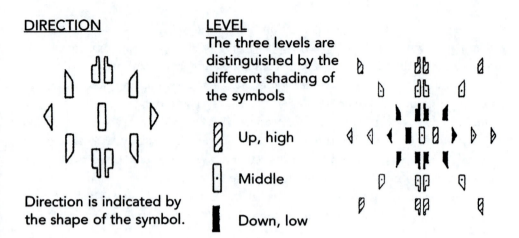

Direction is indicated by the shape of the symbol.

LEVEL

The three levels are distinguished by the different shading of the symbols

Up, high

Middle

Down, low

Fig. 2. Direction was shown by these symbols being placed along the relevant part of the staff, and timing by the length of each symbol. (Reproduced with kind permission from *Labanotation* by Ann Hutchinson, Oxford University Press, 1970.)

THE BODY SIGNS

The Joint Signs

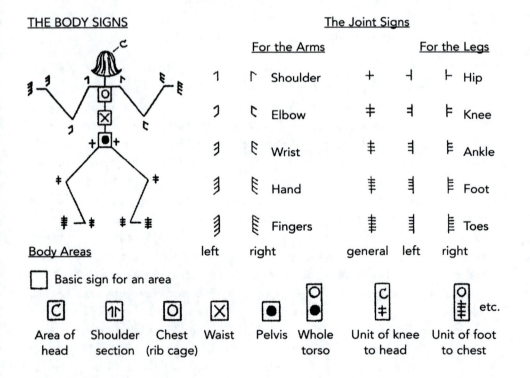

For the Arms

				For the Legs		
1	Shoulder	+	⊣	⊢	Hip
	Elbow				Knee
	Wrist				Ankle
	Hand				Foot
	Fingers				Toes
left	right	general	left	right

Body Areas

☐ Basic sign for an area

Area of head | Shoulder section | Chest (rib cage) | Waist | Pelvis | Whole torso | Unit of knee to head | Unit of foot to chest | etc.

Fig. 3. The basic body signs. (Reproduced with kind permission from *Labanotation* by Ann Hutchinson, Oxford University Press, 1970.)

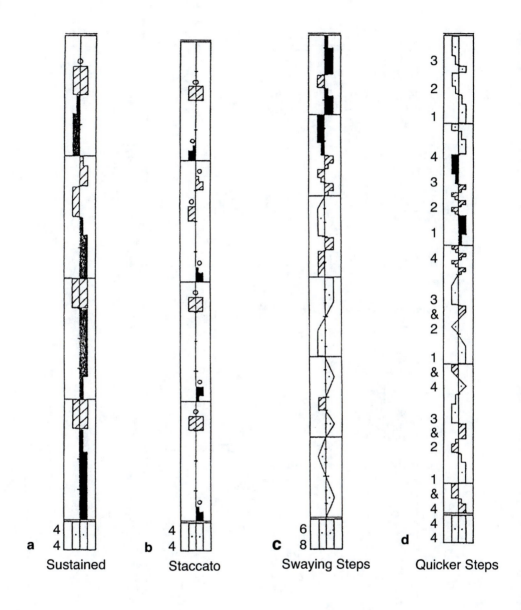

Fig. 4. Contrasts in the Use of Rhythms. [a] and [b] are the same pattern but [a] is legato while [b] is staccato. In [d] two steps lead into the first measure, these form two upbeats on counts of "4, &". Rhythm or timing is shown by horizontal lines marking off the beat. (Reproduced with kind permission from *Labanotation* by Ann Hutchinson, Oxford University Press, 1970.)

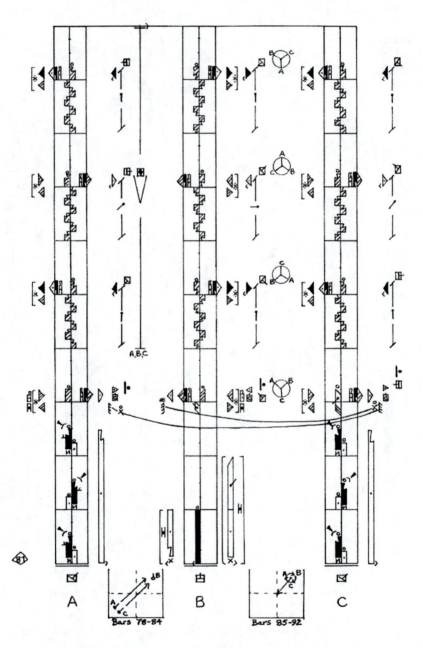

An example of notation for three dancers. Kinetography Laban Dance Score by Sally Archbutt for "Once I Had Laughter" by Hettie Loman. First performed at the Library Theatre, Manchester, UK in 1950.

The corollary to this is that analysis of individual movement was also possible, and this in turn lead to the discovery that a person's individual pattern of movement is a reliable blueprint of their personal abilities, practical, personal and social. What is doubtful is that Laban's heritage in this respect has ever had the attention and validation necessary to establish it on a sound and scientific basis firmly in the public domain. The application of his theories in business management and in therapy has been remarkable and hugely significant. But it has necessarily been for the most part commercial and piecemeal. This is in no way to denigrate the leading disciples and exponents of Laban in the industrial field, notably such men of originality and vision as F.C. Lawrence and Warren Lamb. Through them Laban's theories have been tested in the hardest environment. It is simply to regret that so much of such great and fascinating value having been discovered, is in danger of being lost without taking its place in the mainstream of human knowledge.

Interest and research into the work of Rudolf Laban is carried out extensively, but somehow remains a largely academic exercise carried out among like-minded people. His name is still connected primarily with dance although in many cases the philosophical basis of his theories of Choreutics and Eukinetics have been left behind in dance education. In the application of his work to movement observation and notation in industry, however, these theories are as integral today as they were originally. But this aspect of his heritage is known to relatively few people, when it could be so useful in so many fields.

All this was in the future. As Hitler and his Nazi party gathered strength, so was Laban at the peak of his power, a prolific teacher of dance, a choreographer, and the designer of massive pageants at civic festivals. Mary Wigman and Kurt Jooss, two of his star pupils, had set up their own schools using their Laban training. In the hands of other disciples, "the scribes", Labanotation was steadily being developed and refined. Germany led the world in modern dance and Laban was at the leading edge of dance in Germany. Students came from other countries to be trained there, including students from English teacher training colleges who visited the studios of Wigman, Jooss and Laban. Ironically it was to be the impending war which would broaden the application of Laban's ideas from expressive dance to an analytical tool.

The Elmhirsts at Dartington, courtesy of the Dartington Hall archive.

CHAPTER TWO

LABAN'S WAR EFFORT

HIS ARRIVAL IN ENGLAND – DARTINGTON

Laban was appointed Choreographer and Director of Movement to the Prussian State Theatres in 1930, a position he held till 1934. With the boundaries of Eastern Europe re-drawn after 1918 his nationality, which he changed more than once, was always a problem, and he applied for German nationality. This was eventually granted in 1935, and in 1936 he was put in charge of part of the dance arrangements for the 'Hitler' Olympics. He was at the height of his eminence in German dance, his name was known throughout Europe and he had friends in high places.

Even as his fortunes soared there was evidence of his eventual fall from honour. The glittering spectacle of 1000 dancers in 22 groups he had arranged for the opening of one of the Olympic venues, the Dietrich Eckart building, should have been a crowning glory, but was cancelled after Goebbels and Hitler watched the dress rehearsal. It was deemed to promote Laban's ideas rather than National Socialism.

An incident shortly after would not have helped his prospects either but it illustrates his spirit. At the International Dance Competition, part of the Olympic year celebrations, Laban was to award the prize on the final night, but had been instructed by Goebbels it should go to the German team trained by Mary Wigman. Laban's reaction was to give everyone a prize. For a while he survived, but his contract with the State Theatres had not been renewed and he was gradually stripped of all other posts including his teaching permit. With no prospects of income and in poor health he had to consider emigrating.

It seems a pity that after such a passage of time there are now people intent on investigating Laban for suspected collaboration with the Nazis. Against such an accusation the reality of the situation has to be considered. Laban was already in post as Choreographer to the State Theatres based in Berlin when Hitler came to power in 1933, and was for the first time able to put his dreams of community dance truly into practice free from the usual monetary anxieties. It is unlikely that a person so utterly engrossed in himself and his own work would put much store by the political hysteria round him in Berlin. His artistic aspirations transcended and ignored politics. Again the analysis recently made of Laban by Warren Lamb [Appendix 1] throws an interesting light on his behaviour. Laban was a visionary bursting with creative ideas, and these ideas he immediately converted into action. There was no intermediate stage of evaluating his actions, working out the consequences. His profile is that of a totally engrossed and apolitical artist. It is also interesting that his work in Berlin does not appear to have received the acclaim he achieved elsewhere. This was partly a reaction to the constrictions put upon him by a regime increasingly obsessed with control. While the position gave him prestige and an income, he regarded such work as routine compared with his work through his schools. Again in *A Life for Dance* written in 1935, he described accepting guest engagements at various theatres as something which was "only acceptable to me as a temporary measure".

Perhaps the only loyalty Laban understood was to his work. A comparison can be drawn with the conductor Fürtwangler, Director of the Berlin Philharmonic among other positions, with whom Laban would have worked on occasion, and whose predicament is examined in Ronald Harwood's play *Taking Sides*. The Berlin Philharmonic Orchestra was described to Ronald Harwood by George Solti as Fürtwangler's 'jewel'. Was the position with the State Theatres perhaps Laban's 'jewel'? To walk away from such vehicles of expression would have been treacherous both to their art and to the artists in their care. Fürtwangler stayed and continued to conduct for Hitler; at the same time he employed and saved the lives of many Jews, only to undergo a cruel de-Nazification after the war. Laban ploughed on, mostly toeing the line just enough to escape criticism, and probably turning a blind eye to matters which incensed others, behaving as he had always behaved. Women friends close to the party for whatever reason protected him. One was Marie Luise Lieschke, a wealthy friend of party members who kept his notation association going throughout, and the other was Winifred Wagner, daughter-in-law of his favourite composer and an overt Nazi. To Laban no doubt their political affiliations were of little consequence compared with their contribution to his notation and to music.

Eventually his luck ran out as more militaristic factions who saw the liberal arts as superfluous and degenerate took control. His closest colleagues and pupils had already escaped, mostly to Britain, and his schools had been purged of non-Aryans. It was increasingly difficult to carry on working.

Laban could never be applauded as a person who opposed the Nazis, but neither can he be seen as a collaborator. On the other hand he did expel Jews from his company when required and that could certainly be construed as anti-Semitic.

Rudolf Laban in his study at Dartington, 1938

What is more likely is that in all this as in most of his personal life Laban was consistent only in being blithely amoral and expedient. At such times many people are. If his actions were perceived as proactive towards the Nazis it is extraordinary that he was later allowed not only to work in industry in Britain, but to work in sensitive industries requiring special government clearance for visits. His contemporaries in the dance world would surely also have expressed their disapproval, and there is no evidence that Laban was shunned by colleagues who were earlier refugees; the evidence in fact points in exactly the opposite direction.

Fleeing Germany in 1937, he went to Paris where he lived in penury until seen there by an ex-pupil, Lisa Ullman. She had arrived in England some years earlier with Kurt Jooss and Sigurd Leeder who had been invited to relocate their dance school at Dartington in Devon, home of the Elmhirst family. When Ullman reported Laban's situation back to Jooss he immediately secured from the Elmhirsts an invitation for Laban to join him, and in very poor health Laban landed at Southampton in the winter of 1938.

Jooss had trained under Laban at the National Theatre in Mannheim, and travelled with him to Hamburg in 1922 to become his principal dancer and assistant. He was later director of the Munster Stadttheater and formed his own company. Jooss and Mary Wigman are the two personalities most responsible for carrying Laban's dance to the public in Europe, the USA and Japan. In 1933 he was

Rudolf Laban and Kurt Jooss

ordered to expel all Jews from his employment and rather than comply, fled with Leeder first to Holland then to England.

The Dartington Hall estate had been acquired by Dorothy and Leonard Elmhirst in 1925. In its ramshackle medieval buildings and beautiful parkland, they saw a place where they could put into practice the social, cultural, agricultural and industrial ideals they had formed during travels in America and India. Their doctrines combined self-sufficiency, personal responsibility, and a blending of art and industry. Self-sufficiency extended to Dartington having its own power station as well as its own school and teacher-training college. In the arts the Foundation has become best known for its music school, and in industry for Dartington glass.

For Laban it was a haven and must have taken his mind back to the happy and fruitful times spent in Ascona, dancing to the rising sun or the full moon. He might well have thought of pursuing the same ends at Dartington, and undoubtedly, despite being ill when he arrived, he soon recovered sufficiently to become involved with teaching. His main concern by now, however, was to develop his research into Eukinetics.

His interest in Eukinetics sprang from his earlier cultivation of movement choirs. He believed it was important to enable people to dance in their own individual way, to express their own uniqueness, to discover the richness of their own Effort and by this to combat the ravages of industrialisation. Awareness of Eukinetics could revive a person's sense of their individuality and this is what restoring man's dignity meant to Laban. He dreamt of new forms of folk and social dance being created in the Western world to compensate for the degrading machine work threatening to make robots out of people. His achievements and his following were already immense. A modern folk movement in Germany related to industrial life had burgeoned, and dance had taken an equal place in cultural life. Its stultification at the hands of the Nazis who favoured rigorous body culture was one of the many tragedies of World War II.

When asked in the 1950s how his interest in movement in industry began, Laban dated it to 1929 when he was directing the Festive Procession of Crafts and Industries in Vienna. "The cortege was four miles long, with 10,000 people taking part, and over 400 crafts represented. … This gave me the opportunity to go into factories and workshops to study their basic movements." [Olive Moore, Scope Magazine, Oct. 1954] During these studies for the pageant, he developed his theory of National Rhythm. It is easy to visualise the difference between national dance rhythms of say, the Greeks or the Irish, the Polynesians or the Zulus. According to Laban these represent a difference in rhythm of the national way of life. He told how he talked to a travelling blacksmith, who claimed that whilst the horseshoes he made in each country were exactly the same in the end, they were made in each country to a different rhythm equating with the national dance rhythm – the waltz in Alsace, the tarantella in Italy and the reel in Scotland.

Laban also claimed in the same interview that as soon as he talked to people in the workplace they came to him with problems which arose from the unnatural way they had to work. Centres were opened in his name all over Germany and Europe where artisans could come for advice on the stresses and strains of their occupations. In this might be seen the seed of the consultancy work he was to develop in England first on the shop floor and later with management.

At Dartington Laban found a sympathetic environment receptive to all the contemporary philosophical ideals he had left behind. Here he was prepared to put his fascination with the theatre on one side in order to pursue his interest in Effort at work. Fortuitously two people ideally fitted to assist him in both aspects of his work were there and he formed enduring friendships with both of them. These were Lisa Ullmann and F.C. Lawrence.

LISA ULLMANN AND EDUCATION

Lisa Ullmann left her job as trainer to the Ballets Jooss company to look after the ailing Laban and to help him with his work. She proved a talented teacher, although she was often criticised for a lack of personal originality and for being simply a mouthpiece for Laban. Nevertheless they were an extremely effective team and she was to care for him possessively for the rest of his life. A teachers' training college was already part of the Dartington Foundation, and Laban and Ullmann soon interested the teachers there in dance and movement. A series of summer schools and short courses much the same as those which Laban and his pupils had held in Germany, were soon underway at Dartington, at Bedford College and at other centres. The amount they achieved is remarkable given Laban's poor health and the enormous difficulties for two "alien" subjects to move around England during wartime. Out of these courses eventually grew the Art of Movement Studios in Manchester in 1946 and later in Addlestone, Surrey. The courses at the latter were recognised by the Ministry of Education and were eventually incorporated into the Goldsmith College, London University curriculum after Lisa Ullmann retired in 1973. The Art of Movement Studio stayed at Addlestone till 1976 when it moved to the Laban Centre in New Cross, London. Although Laban was the driving force of the Studio, he held no formal title there, and the Director was always Lisa Ullmann.

Interest in physical education was increasing in Britain at this time. The League of Health, Margaret Morris and Medau were all part of the current trend. Dance schools in England had taken a great interest in German dance [or Central European Dance as it was now preferred to call it] during the twenties and thirties. Many English dancers had trained in Europe at some time, particularly with Mary Wigman and many of these were from the Bedford Physical Training College. It was fortunate for English dance probably that refugees like Laban, Ullmann and Jooss had fallen foul of the Nazi regime, since this made it acceptable for English dancers to take an interest in their work during the war years.

Into this scenario ideas of encouraging more expressive use of physical education time, of allowing children to move more freely rather than copying set moves, found their place. There was of course debate as to whether it was suitable for boys, and whether it fitted into dance or 'gym' on a timetable, but it became accepted that healthy physical self-expression was integral to a healthy body and balanced mind. The Ministry of Education published two manuals "Moving and Growing" and "Planning a Programme" which showed photographs of children of different ages in wonderful dance-like activity and interesting groupings, quite unlike anything previously in a PE syllabus.

Laban is still implicit in movement education. In training colleges his theories of space, weight and time are taught as part of training for PE teachers. In the 1940s his teaching coincided with a move away from teaching by rote to child-centred teaching. In all arts subjects, especially in PE, children were encouraged into self-expression and for many years rigorous keep-fit and competitive sport were unfashionable. More recently there has been a move to reinstate discipline and competition on the sports field and to generally move back to subject-based teaching, but the influence of Laban is still there and good teachers will find a way to make subject and child meet. His theories are still taught in dance and theatre schools, and are used in training for art and dance therapy.

LABAN AND F.C. LAWRENCE

Meanwhile Laban's relationship with F.C. Lawrence had drawn him into work which was to be his "bread and butter" and would lay the foundation for the application of his ideas to movement in industry. Lawrence was not on paper the most obvious candidate to partner Laban. He was an accountant and engineer, while Laban was an artist and a philosopher. He was one of the first management consultants in the UK, having set up an office in Manchester in 1923, and had developed the innovative concept of "marginal costing". Lawrence was on a consultancy assignment at Dartington for his company Paton, Lawrence & Co. in 1942 to do with the administration of Dartington Rural Industries when he met Laban roaming around observing the workers' Efforts and offering guidance on how they could do their jobs more effectively and with less strain to their physique.

An immediate bond was formed between the two men, Lawrence becoming so attached to Laban as to hang on his every word. During World War 1 Lawrence had suffered horrific experiences as an army officer, the effects of which, perhaps together with other personality problems, were addressed by Laban when they first met. Laban's healing influence, testified to by many people at all stages of his career, was highly successful for Lawrence. He felt indebted to Laban for the rest of his life, elevating him almost to the status of a god. Of course Laban loved it.

Laban's capacity as a healer arose not from any mystical talent or 'laying on of hands' but from his penetrating recognition of the essence of an individual's personality. It was an ability born out of his fascination with people and from his prevailing interest throughout his career in spiritual motivation. Like so many others, usually women, Lawrence felt here was someone who thoroughly understood him and on whose every word he was prepared to act. It made him feel much more of a whole person, more sure of himself, realising a greater personal potential.

Laban's later disciple, Warren Lamb, sees this ability to understand people as an intuitive use of his skills in movement analysis which he imparted to his closest pupils. But he too acknowledges the magnetic charisma of Laban which had so many of his students feeling that they were his favoured pupil and that they had a special mission to promote his work. Laban had a remarkable physical presence, large and rugged with a fine head and eyes that missed nothing. According again to Olive Moore, he had "genius without arrogance, strength with understanding … the exacting patience of the artist and scientist and an inability to suffer fools gladly".

According to Warren Lamb who probably came to know Laban better than anyone other than Lisa Ullman, Laban's pride of bearing was evident in everything he did. Lamb describes how, although Laban enjoyed enormous prestige in Germany, in post-war England he was teaching in a drab slum area of Manchester, and living in a modest terraced house. "Yet wherever he went, even among people who did not know his background, he was received as someone of weight and substance. He made pride seem a virtue rather than one of the deadly sins."

Throughout his life Laban had this charismatic effect on those around him and was able to ask great sacrifices in time and effort from his many disciples. Warren Lamb's recent analysis of Laban's movement pattern explains the way in which this charisma was made up. He was able then to take on huge workloads, to initiate many projects at once, and let others pick up the pieces, fill in the gaps, trim the edges and deal with the practicalities. If as he regularly did, he fell ill and disappeared off the scene for a few months, his loyal disciples carried the torch for him. In wartime England it is remarkable how much he and Lisa Ullmann achieved. They were both subject to travel restrictions, and travel at best at that time was difficult, yet throughout the war they undertook work in one part of England after another and somehow the journeys worked, the appointments were kept, reports were delivered.

The work Lawrence invited him to help with appealed to Laban who immediately saw his chance to further his theories on the social importance of understanding movement. He saw, too, an opportunity to "do his bit" for the national war effort of the country which had taken him in. Lawrence meanwhile recognised the greater efficiency of being able to annotate movement. Time and Motion Study was currently fashionable as the means of increasing productivity and at first glance it might have appeared that Laban's concern with the way people performed tasks bore a close relation to it. Nothing could be further from the truth, of course, and Lawrence in fact was already becoming dissatisfied with Time and Motion Study, the aim of which was to reduce worker movements to the minimum. This was done by the careful arrangement of machinery, conveyor belts, supply of units or whatever, and by devising an exact pattern of movement for everyone to follow. All this was exactly what Laban saw as the worst by-product of mechanisation, the subjugation of individuality, and Lawrence had come to the realisation that human beings were not so tractable. In the companies they worked in together Tyresoles and Mars are two of the best documented. In both Laban's concern is entirely with showing the individual operator how they might work more fluently with less strain on their body and more enjoyment of the task. In this way, he believed, they would increase not only their productivity but also their self-esteem.

In June 1942 the Dartington News of the Day announced that Part I of a course called *Rhythmic Movement in Industry* would be held with Mr Laban and Miss Ullmann there for a few weeks. Parts II and III were to follow during July. They would be looking at agricultural and factory processes it said, and giving classes in basic exercises. The exercises later became known as the Laban/Lawrence Industrial Rhythm, and were designed to help people work more comfortably and more efficiently. At Dartington they were concerned with such work as planting cabbages, lifting potatoes, pruning fruit trees, thinning beetroot, and filling sacks with peas. A report in The News Chronicle in October 1942 reported the technique whereby "Factory workers are to be taught rhythmic movements by which maximum results can be achieved from the minimum physical effort. ... This they say will increase efficiency and pleasure in work, and lessen fatigue."

LILT IN LABOUR

During the war women often had to do work normally done by men in some crucial industries, and this provided Laban with the ideal opportunity to test his theories on the correct use of Effort. A case in point was the Tyresoles company where women had to handle the heavy duty tyres taken in for re-treading [an important exercise during the years of the blockade].

Lawrence, sending a suggested programme of training to the company wrote, "you will realise that in both speed of Application and in refinement of results, the Laban method offers a very considerable advance upon any existing Training Methods". Lawrence, Laban, Ullmann and Sylvia Bodmer – another Laban disciple who had also arrived in England – were all involved in devising and implementing a training programme, one of the first of a type which Laban and Lawrence would offer many companies to improve productivity.

The training programme involved firstly a detailed study of the tasks the women had to perform in all the processes of handling the tyres. The parts of the body used in these tasks were noted and movement analyses were made of the people performing them. Special exercises were then devised to strengthen their bodies for the operations, and more fluent and rhythmic ways of performing the tasks were suggested. The exercises may have been designed to build up essential muscle strength, but they had nothing to do with the old-fashioned drill then taught in schools, nor with the modern concept of "pumping iron". Instead they took the form of rhythmic dance-like movements.

Selected women were given two three-quarter hour movement training sessions each day for a week. They were then to instruct their colleagues in methods of handling the tyres, and in exercises to tone themselves for the work. The aim was to increase the continuous lifting power of the average worker from 45lbs to an incredible 80lbs. This entailed exercises designed to develop an impressive array of physical qualities; strength, a firm stance, positioning of the centre of gravity, endurance, sensitiveness of touch, quick decisions and easy use of the hands. General preparatory exercises were designed for each part of the training. For firm stance for example, these were: bending and stretching the knees, bending and stretching the trunk in all directions, exercises for the shoulders, girdle and arms, exercises for the forearms and hands – grasping and scattering.

The exercises were then adapted to the different tasks the women had to perform in the repair shop, for example, or on the buffing machine, or for the vulcanising procedure. In all cases the exercises paid particular attention to respiration, tension, relaxation and the rhythmical flow of movements. Most important it also laid down compensatory exercises to counteract the strain of the work. The Swinging Scales were built into the training to lift the tyres with a swing, but rather than give them that name the word 'lilt' was used, and the training method for women was known as Lilt in Labour. The project reflected the philosophical basis Laban brought to all aspects of movement: that in industry just as much as in dance, movement should be a dignified, graceful and joyful experience.

It must all have been strange stuff to women in Britain at that time, and courageous of the employers to take it on board. In May 1942 Ullmann reported that the women were enjoying the training and showing beneficial results. In the same month Lawrence had to apply for a special travel permit for Laban, to travel to a protected area where Tyresoles work was carried out.

Tyresoles also saw the first industry-specific training manual for use by the company's instructors. Later in the same year Time and Motion men were being trained at Hoover, and work was undertaken at Fort Dunlop, Birmingham, and at the W.C. Holmes & Co. foundry.

A significant development at W.C. Holmes was that the workers were selected for various tasks according to their aptitudes. Laban and Lawrence devised tests for speed, skill, attitude and reliability appropriate to each part of the assembly line, and moved workers to their optimum position according to their abilities in the tests. The process of moving towards an analysis of aptitude through movement analysis had begun and it was based on Laban's fundamental but simple premise that certain people will have aptitude for certain jobs, according to their very individual and favoured way of moving. The essential tool, which made these analyses possible of course, was Labanotation.

In the same year, 1942, Laban and Lawrence jointly published *Industrial Rhythm*. This set out Laban's rather mystical and philosophical beliefs on movement at work, and these were translated by Lawrence into terms more palatable to British management. The book was well received and it had been a fruitful year.

The next year, 1943, a note from Lawrence to Laban in April instructed him to pay Jean Newlove £10 for her work at Mars. Jean Newlove had joined Laban as a dancer, but like all his pupils was not allowed to specialise, and was sent wherever the work was, in this case to the Mars factory. The chocolate-coated Mars Bar and its sister Starry Ways were part of a survival pack carried by combatants such as parachutists during the war and was prized for its energy-giving qualities. Work in the Mars factory was definitely related to the War Effort.

Mars Bars had ridges on top, and no wrapping machine had been designed at that time which left the ridges intact, so each one had to be wrapped by hand. Turnover and absenteeism among the female workforce was high and morale poor, and Paton, Lawrence & Co were given the task of improving productivity.

Prior to Laban's arrival the workers had been trained by Time and Motion experts in the most efficient hand and finger movements necessary to wrap the Bar. They had to grasp the Bar with just enough pressure to lift it without smashing it, place it on the wrapper and, with deft finger movements, fold the wrap-

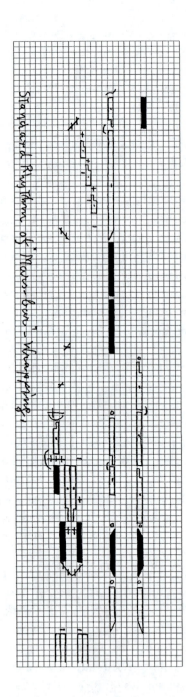
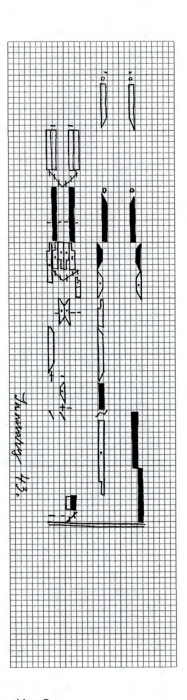

Taken from Laban's original script for wrapping a Mars Bar

per to cover the Bar before putting it back onto the conveyor with the wrapper securely in place. This sequence of movements had been devised to cut out any time-wasting, unnecessary movement, and was taught in exactly the same way to every worker.

Of course the workers, all women of different ages, sizes, shapes and characters, found their own ways of trying to deal with the stresses this caused as best they could, which in many cases was not very well. Neck, shoulder and backache were common. Time spent pausing to rest aching muscles meant less production and accordingly less pay for the workers. Most of the women put themselves under great stress to keep going and to earn as much as possible.

The preliminary study by Laban shows his radically different approach to problem-solving. He identified 'Tiredness, Cramp and Boredom' as the disincentives to this piecework. These problems he said resulted from 'the exaggerated participation of the upper part of the body, the restriction on single joints – shoulders, elbows, wrists and fingers, and the permanently bent head impeding free-breathing.'

Laban and Newlove were given permission to take the workers away from their conveyor belt for fifteen minutes mid-morning and mid-afternoon. Laban had worked out how the particular type of light, precise movements of the hands combined with the flexibility necessary for wrapping the Mars Bar, could be performed without strain. He devised a system of compensatory exercises and improved the actual wrapping action so that it merged into a whole body movement. For example, initially reaching to grasp the Bar from the belt was combined with a change of weight from one foot to the other to merge it with the delicate grasping of the Bar. During training classes the workers were made aware of the relevant movement qualities and encouraged to find their own way of making the merger. The wrapping action was also developed into a flexible movement involving the upper part of the body and legs. Involvement of the whole body in this way sustained and even enhanced the efficiency of the hand and finger movements over a long period.

The company was naturally anxious that having the workers away from the belt for a total of half an hour every day would reduce production, but Laban claimed that production would rise. This proved to be the case and by a significant margin. Not only was the company happy (paying immediately their £250 fee), but the workers were much happier too and many less incidences of strain were reported. The training classes were like dance classes and each worker enjoyed experiment-

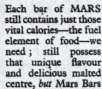

Mars wartime advertisement.

ing with how she could find her own way of incorporating whole bodily movement into the tasks they had to perform.

As part of the whole consultancy exercise an explanatory circular was sent to the workers in January 1943 entitled "What we would like to tell you about Lilt in Labour". They were not being required to work harder, it said, but they would, through the changes have greater satisfaction in their work and this would lead to greater production. The exercises would relieve tension and cramp, and they would find their "personality becoming stronger and freer". The wartime spirit is captured in the exhortation, which introduced the circular:

"As food becomes scarcer and less varied, Mars Bars and Starry Ways become more and more welcome and help to keep up the peckers of the people.

"The fighting forces, men and women, look forward to them in parcels and in the NAAFIs, especially abroad.

"But above all, the kiddies search the Shops for bars.

"If it is only for them, your job in making Mars Bars and Starry Ways is one of the greatest importance.

"It is these "extras" that make it easier to stand the strain and really makes us fit to work, to fight, and to play the game.

"As the fighting comes nearer home – that second front – Mars Bars and Starry Ways will play even a greater part in the War Effort."

Progress was not automatically smooth. Many of the workers were called up or moved away, and Jean Newlove was ill for a while. But eventually the programme was underway and productivity improved as staff turnover and absenteeism decreased.

There may be some comparison here with the Japanese practice of having everyone exercise in the mornings, or the Chinese way of having everyone do Tai Chi before they start work, but Laban's pioneering work in Industrial Rhythm was very different. He claimed that the same set of exercises could not be used universally; every operation needs its own set of compensatory exercises, just as much as each individual needs to find their own way of performing a task.

This is a lesson we would do well to take on board today. While conveyor belt operations are mostly a thing of the past, other unnaturally stressful occupations have taken their place. For example there is currently a recognised need for schemes to relieve the stresses of focussing on a computer screen, and using a mouse and keyboard for hours at a time. It is estimated that 200,000 keyboard operators in Britain at present suffer from RSI (Repetitive Strain Injury), a condition defined by the BMA as "an over-use injury causing muscular spasms and swelling of the joints, tendons and ligaments". Together with back-pain, RSI is thought to cost business in Britain alone in the region of £2 billion a year. Keyboard operators may be one of the most usual sufferers, but RSI is a condition afflicting people in a wide range of repetitive jobs including musicians, check-out operators and even more unlikely occupations. In the USA the highest number of RSI cases are found in meat-packing and car manufacturing. There keyboard operators accounted for only 12% of cases in 1992.

In 1993 Judge Prosser, in a case brought against Reuters by a sub-editor, claimed that RSI was an imaginary condition, and that "sufferers need to get a grip on themselves". A few weeks earlier a woman bank clerk, also claiming to suffer from RSI, had her disability allowance discontinued and was told to consider "light work" such as food-tasting or nude modelling. Whatever the validity or justice of these cases, many since have resulted in substantial payments.

Working at modern keyboards requires a very light touch compared with old-fashioned typewriters where one had to pause to wind in the paper or to move the carriage across. In theory all that one now needs to move for perhaps hours at a time is the hands or perhaps even just the fingers and eyes. Even with good seating and support the hands will become isolated from the rest of the body, and as shown in the Mars example in 1943, should periodically be incorporated into a whole bodily adjustment. So prevalent is the use of computers now, and from such an early age, that this simple lesson in learning to live with them is one that probably should be part of the school curriculum.

Research in Australia found that children as young as ten were suffering RSI symptoms, and in England the Body Action Campaign is making a special study of the problem for schoolchildren here. All this would have perhaps been unnecessary if the lessons available half a century earlier had been taken on board.

In 1942 Lawrence wrote to Dr Slater concerning the work to be carried out at Dartington Sawmills: "...we do not give training in specific operations. We train women [or men] to develop muscles, nerves and body features such as lever, pendulum, centre of gravity etc together with mental characteristics such as direction, precision and orientation, in such a way that they can use them to the best advantage in their work and control their actions, thus avoiding strain and other injurious affects and eventually that they might find greater enjoyment in their occupation."

By the end of the war in 1945, Laban's reputation was established on both its educational and industrial platforms. He himself would not draw this clear distinction any more than he would allow his students to do so. In dance he aimed to 'form right movement habits and to engender a co-operative spirit', a philosophical approach which could apply equally well in industry. Dancers and workers alike were encouraged to develop a sense of rhythm, by which he meant Effort rhythm, around which the Shape of their movement would arise. The laws of movement were laws of nature, the space in which we move is the shape of a pure crystal, the effort lines within it the facets within the crystal which he found so deeply inspirational.

CHAPTER THREE

SHAPE AND EFFORT

WARREN LAMB AND THE ART OF MOVEMENT STUDIO

Laban's work with Paton Lawrence & Co continued and gained pace after 1945. When the following year a student called Warren Lamb joined the Art of Movement Studio in Manchester and showed particular ability to observe and record movement, Laban very soon put him to work. This was not unusual. Although students mostly arrived at the doors of the Art of Movement Studio with some ambition to go on the stage, Laban refused to let them specialise. Everyone had to experience movement from every angle and this included observation and notation in industry as well as expressive dance. Nevertheless it gradually became clear that Warren D. Lamb was destined to be the person who would carry Laban's work forward in the industrial field.

Working in factories had already established the principle that each person should find their own way of performing even simple operative tasks, and furthermore that certain people were better suited to particular tasks, even positions in a team, than others. Warren Lamb would develop this concept from the seeds sown by Laban and Lawrence. It lead to the discovery that each person's movement pattern, developed in early childhood, is as individual as their fingerprint or their DNA. By identifying and analysing this movement pattern it is possible to predict how the person will react and inter-react in any given situation, not simply in operative tasks but in personal relationships, management positions, and anything requiring the assessment of personality. To take his work this far, as Warren Lamb has, was completely in accord with Laban's basic philosophy that man's dignity and individuality should be protected in an increasingly mechanised world.

Warren Lamb was born in Wallasey in 1923, and after attending grammar school was encouraged by his parents into a position with Lloyds Bank. As soon as he was old enough he enlisted in the Royal Navy, and saw active service in the Mediterranean. In 1946 his interest in amateur theatre led him to attend a Modern Dance Holiday Course at Dartington run by Lisa Ullmann and Laban, and immediately, to his parents' consternation, he decided to abandon the Bank and join the newly-formed Art of Movement Studio in Manchester. It was an unlikely step for a person from his background, but from the start Laban recognised Lamb's natural

Warren Lamb as a young man.

ability. Although he had undoubted talent as a dancer, he had even greater skills as an observer of movement.

His skill perhaps came from what Lamb calls a highly developed Kinaesthetic Sense. This is something he sees as a natural addition to the five senses. In a dancer there would be a well-developed Kinaesthetic Intelligence because their minds should function in close affinity with the form and pattern of their physical activity, but this might not be an automatic, intuitive appreciation of the flow of movement. A conclusion Lamb came to early in his time with Laban was that dancing ability or physical training and a heightened Kinaesthetic Sense do not necessarily go together. In fact a remarkable sensitivity to movement is often found in people who have never trained in dance, drama or sport.

Measurement of intelligence is an accepted procedure, but as an indication of potential performance in a given job it is misleading if the person has a low application to action. We all know at least one person who is incredibly intelligent but physically hopelessly uncoordinated. Measurement of what he would later call the Action Quotient of an individual should, he claims, be complementary to the Intelligence Quotient in order to know what a person can achieve. A traditional Spanish proverb apparently makes similar claims:

High Intelligence + High Action = Leaders of the world

High Intelligence + Low Action = the Academics

Low Intelligence + Low Action = those needed to do humble jobs

Low Intelligence + High Action = these people menace world stability

In November 1946 Warren Lamb presented himself at the Art of Movement Studio, recently opened by Laban and Ullman in a war-damaged area of Manchester. His war service gratuity of £62 had paid for one and a half terms' tuition which he expected to lead to a career as a dancer. The Studio was in a shabby room over a noisy printing shop. But there in the next three years it was the scene for him of more creativity, vision and excitement than he could have found in any of the better-appointed dance schools.

Not that this was evident on his first day. As instructed, he appeared wearing swim pants and shivering with cold. The teacher was Joan Goodrich, recently retired from working as a Physical Education Inspector for the Ministry of Education. She taught a Sicilian folk dance, and was strict, demanding and formal, and Warren Lamb began to doubt his decision.

The next morning was better. Geraldine Stephenson, a graduate of Bedford College and still working today as a choreographer, gave a vigorous class based purely on Laban's principles. Ballet dancers, of course, start the day with a specialised system of barre exercises, followed by practice of those movements specific to ballet. Laban, like Noverre several centuries earlier, saw classical ballet as restrictive. If the only way to dance were ballet then most people would be eliminated because of their physique and their inability to achieve a standard at the specialised techniques. Gerry's class was designed around a clear theme of movement and it was obvious that this was one theme out of a total 'language' of themes which would become increasingly obvious as time went on.

A theme in movement is similar to a theme in music. It can be introduced, developed, repeated at a different level, associated with a subsidiary theme. It can be used either to challenge the student's creativity or as a technical exercise or both. A training class such as this would take a theme and develop it in a physical movement, working towards perfect precision of the movement whilst encouraging the student to think creatively.

Recognising that it is the student's body which is the instrument, a certain amount of static muscle-stretching had to be part of the training in order to avoid injury. Students had to have a reasonably well-tuned body just as the language student has to have a reasonable vocabulary or the music student a good instrument. Curt Sachs said in *The History of Dance*, "Dance is unique among the arts because the creator and the thing created are one and the same." For this reason movement can only be learnt by its practice, not by observing or reading about it.

This does not mean that the student needs a wonderful physique. The group of students Warren Lamb joined at the Art of Movement Studio in 1946 were almost all apart from him, physically highly educated, having trained in dance or physical education or both. Later, however, people came from a range of backgrounds and they would be the first to admit that their bodies were not well-tuned or supple. They may have been attracted to movement study in the hope that they would become more so, but their interest was primarily a fascination with the subject itself. The approach was quite different from a traditional dance training where the student would be interested in a particular type of dance and would choose their school accordingly. Laban's principle that a student studied movement for three years and only then chose his or her vocation, applied equally to aspiring dancers. After that time they would be much better able to select the type of dance to which they were most suited and bring to it a much richer experience.

Laban sought to develop the Kinaesthetic Sense in his students, to show them that movement consisted of Shape and Effort, design in Space, rather than a movement of parts of the body.

CHOREUTICS

The third class dealt with Choreutics, the architectural element in movement. Warren Lamb describes Choreutics as the sculptural shape which would emerge if small jets giving off vapour trails were attached to all parts of the body and the resulting shape could be seen. It might appear elongated, flattened, or composed of short angular lines, but it would not have any similarity to the body which created it.

Laban had done a vast amount of research in this field, variously called Choreutics, space harmony or the shaping of movement (although more advanced study gives each of these a more specific meaning). He loved to play around with polyhedral forms made from sticks and to catalogue the ways the body can move in space. The icosahedron, a form of 20 equilateral triangles, was his favourite and the scales of movement derived from it were basic to the teaching at the Art of Movement Studio. Laban encouraged his students to read Plato's Timaeus to appreciate the Ancient Greek contribution to this body of knowledge.

In this work Plato postulates that all solids are bounded by surfaces, and that all rectilinear surfaces are composed of triangles. Various combinations of triangles produce the four elements: the cube (earth), the pyramid (fire), the octahedron [air], the icosahedron [water]. The fifth figure, the dodecahedron represented the cosmos and could not be created out of triangles, but was used to "embroider the heavens". To Plato everything was composed of these elements, including the human body, and disease was an imbalance of these elements in the body.

These concepts formed the basis of Laban's mystical view of matter. His related fascination with crystals can perhaps be dated to a time as a teenager when he found himself alone in a cave full of stalactites and stalagmites. The incident is recorded in *A Life for Dance* and describes how he was speechless when he emerged among his father's military colleagues. Crystals were to him the discerning spirit of nature, their planes the planes of movement and the basis for his scales of movement.

Whilst scales can be performed as a discipline, with the teacher making corrections needed, a Choreutic class would usually be based on a particular form and the student would create a study based on that form. Warren Lamb had some prior knowledge of this and found his first class fascinating. Just as, for example,

Chopin plays with a theme in one of his Etudes, so a Choreutics theme could be performed with first one sort of emphasis then another, introduced at a higher level, lead into jumping or use of the floor – an unlimited range of possibilities. It requires a type of creativity which comes easily once the basic concept is understood. Without necessarily having any thought of performance it is interesting to experiment with creating a Choreutic study. It can certainly be physically active, although it is not intended as a "work-out" in the aerobic sense.

EUKINETICS

Some time later Laban introduced a Eukinetic study. This was the line of research on which he concentrated during his later career and in particular in his work in industry. If Choreutics places emphasis on the sculptural quality of movement, then Eukinetics is the intensity and the nature of the effort put into that activity. Laban used Greek rhythms such as Iambus, Trochee, Peon, Dactylus, all of which are more familiar to students of poetry, as examples of the different ways in which we could put effort into movement. When teaching Eukinetics he would guide the class with drumbeats or, more frequently, using his voice with a rhythmic "Rrum tah tah" or similar sounds. Here necessity had been the mother of invention. In his early teaching days in Munich he could not afford musicians for his classes and used drums and percussion, only to find they liberated movement from the restriction of composed music. Soon after joining the Art of Movement Studio, Warren Lamb was dispatched to Paris to meet a composer. There he created dances to various themes of movement and the composer wrote music to match the movement. These motets are still in Warren Lamb's possession and were recently played again to a fascinated group of movement analysts.

All movement of course has both Choreutic and Eukinetic qualities, but one can be more in evidence than the other. Laban tended to concentrate on one at a time when teaching, whereas Warren Lamb in his later career would find it essential to see the two as part of a whole, and the nature of their inter-relationship as crucial to understanding the subject being observed. In industrial observations and later in analysis of movement for senior positions Choreutics and Eukinetics were translated into Shape and Effort, the two fundamental aspects of movement.

In *Effort* which he wrote jointly with Lawrence, Laban developed the theory that it is the Eukinetic aspect of our behaviour which reveals our personality. The Choreutic aspect he associated with a mystical view of our relation to the cosmos and the harmonics of space. He was aware of a relationship between Choreutics and Eukinetics, both of which feature in the diagonal scale, but he seldom referred to them together. In Germany, for example, he and Jooss had made a special study of Eukinetics. Even when adjudicating a dance he would comment on either the Choreutic or Eukinetic aspect, but not on the relationship of one to the other. Warren Lamb describes how Laban and Lisa Ullmann would sit together, he proud, dignified and restrained, she effusive, compassionate and eager. At the end Laban would pronounce, Lisa would jump up and demonstrate. Between the two of them they sent their students away immensely inspired.

Laban was much less effective as a lecturer, when he became rambling and vague, sometimes going on for three hours. Some of his writings ramble on equally. But when he demonstrated he was precision itself. He would instil the 'scales' into his students more rigorously than any music teacher, and these were the daily drill. His teaching of the diagonal scale, for example, would require each movement to have the exact spatial orientation as well as the precise process of effort variation. If the movement required a combination of outwards, upwards and forwards spatial orientation, with an indirect, increasingly light and sustained effort, then all these six processes had to be accurate, no mean feat! Of course, accuracy in this context is relative – there is always some scope for correction. If the student concentrated on getting more upwards orientation then more than likely he or she would lapse on the indirect effort. Laban would jump on this in a flash. Correction of the indirect effort would lead to some other process lapsing. A class could go on for hours, students bathed in sweat and desperately tired, but dredging their last ounces of energy to please the master.

Laban believed this form of drill helped to instil the scales into the bodily instrument and to make them second nature, just as a pianist's practice of scales becomes part of their musicality without need for conscious recall. It occupied most of the morning's teaching and was in contrast to the creative part of the curriculum. Warren Lamb loved it. It seemed to him then as it still does, essential basic training. Once established in the body, movement scales are there for life, just as once we learn to swim or ride a bicycle we never forget.

Most of the students at the Art of Movement Studio had a direct interest in dance. Some were aspiring professional dancers, such as Ronnie Curran, who had been selected by Lisa Ullmann as a dancer with outstanding potential. Compared with him Lamb felt gauche, but it is a testimony to Laban's concept of movement as a "common denominator" that this inferiority soon evaporated, and he appreciated Laban's belief that everyone can dance, we only need to search for the form most appropriate to us. Hence the need to teach a wide variety of styles, even including folk dance.

Within a few months of his joining the Art of Movement Studio, however, it became apparent that Laban had earmarked Lamb primarily as an apprentice for the industrial work begun at Dartington with F.C. Lawrence. This meant that he travelled to factories with the great man and accompanied him on lecture demonstrations where Laban lectured and Lamb demonstrated. He was envied by his fellow students for having Laban so much to himself, and it is probably true that from that time on Lamb was closer to Laban than anyone other than Lisa Ullmann. It is probably also true that no one other than Lamb had the deep first-hand involvement in the transition which was to take place in the industrial application of Laban's research. This was the transition from using movement observation and notation simply to improve efficiency, into using observation of an individual's movement patterns for management and executive selection.

Many of the students from the Art of Movement Studio became teachers. This was unsurprising since Laban to a large extent made them teach each other, a system which verged on exploitation, but also ensured that the "student teacher" had to work hard to be ahead of his contemporaries in his particular subject.

For Warren Lamb that subject was Eukinetics, Effort observation, and he was teaching it a few months after joining the studio. Giving students a uniform understanding of Effort he still admits is a problem to which he has never found an entirely satisfactory solution. Laban had previously taught Effort primarily in a dance context; the problem now was to explain it in terms precise enough for movement observation in ordinary tasks.

If a person hits a table with a thump it is fairly obvious that from the beginning to the end of the action, the Effort – in this case a pressure – varies between light and strong, but this elementary observation does not get you very far. To begin with the observer has to know exactly which parts of the body are involved in the Effort, and when the action began and finished. To truly understand it, the observer should probably copy the action to find out what is going on. He or she would then find the action was in fact part of a 'phrase' of movement all of which it was necessary to observe and record. Lamb's students could therefore often be seen in parks, at railway stations or on building sites, notating the actions of an unsuspecting public.

LAYING DOWN THE RULES FOR MOVEMENT ANALYSIS

At that time Lamb was using Laban's categorisation of Effort into:

1. Functional Movement – movement using an object or tool; or using part of the body as a means of communication, for example waving goodbye or pointing to something.

2. Body Attitude – movement of the body as a whole [others have used this term to describe a fixed state as Laban sometimes did, but to Lamb it was a category of movement].

3. Shadow Movement – movement which flits across the surface of the body, for example a flick of the eyebrows, a twitch of the lips.

This always resulted in argument as to whether a movement might contain two of these categories or even all three. In the work Warren Lamb did in the early days for Paton, Lawrence & Co under Laban's tutelage in the Glaxo company his assessments have "Mainly Shadow Movements" at the top of the page of notations. To a relatively novice observer these would certainly be much easier to see with a degree of certainty, compared with Body Attitude which it would take more practice to confidently identify.

Although Warren Lamb has always been modest about his ability to train students in Effort observation, he easily transmits to others the fascination he himself enjoys in observing and recording movement. Like Laban, Lamb is an inspiring teacher who communicates his subject with enthusiasm and conviction. But whether observation and annotation of Effort is a subject which can be reliably taught to anyone who has not undergone intensive movement training is more problematic, and that is the essential step on which everything else relies. It is relatively easy to see the direction of a movement, for example, but much more difficult to see how the movement goes in that direction, what type of Effort it contains. Add to this the simple leap of credibility required to believe that a person who moves in this way is such and such a type who will be good at performing this type of work, and the management consultant peddling his technique has a mountain to climb; explaining, demonstrating, proving.

Yet Warren Lamb has worked continuously since those early days using his technique of assessment based entirely on the movements he observes in the interviewee. From the beginning he wanted his work to be multi-disciplinary – to apply movement study as a common denominator to many areas of life. Given the difficulty in the early days of gaining acceptance for Laban's ideas, he finds it remarkable that he was able to work in so many fields, be treated with respect and even be paid. Perhaps simply the fact that clients tended to stay with him is in itself testimonial proof of the reliable quality of the results he has always achieved.

The principles Lamb followed then were the same as they are today:

i. Everyone has their individual way of moving.

ii. Because circumstances often prevent people from following their individual way, it is essential that they are aware what their individual way is.

iii. That awareness can be used to avoid foreign movement [forced on you by circumstances] overwhelming individual movement.

iv. Losing touch with an awareness of one's individual movement shows as puppet-like behaviour. Parts of the body appear to move as though pulled by strings and are not integrated into the whole body behaviour.

v. Such forced or puppet-like behaviour is counter-productive in the long term and is associated with some form of stress. Advice should never be concentrated on one part of the body alone, but should be given in the context of body movement as a whole.

THE THREE PLANES OF MOVEMENT — SHAPE

For the purposes of teaching dance, Laban talked in terms of Choreutics and Eukinetics. For teaching movement observation they were given the more everyday descriptions of Shape and Effort, and these are now the established terms. Shape, like Choreutics refers to the architectural qualities of movement, its structure, whilst Effort is the content of the movement, determining whether it is fast or slow, strong or light. Both are observed in a limited number of aspects. For Shape these are three planes, perhaps arbitrarily chosen from the many facets of the icosahedron, but functional. A movement can therefore be seen either as along one of these planes or as a diagonal between two.

They can be described as the Table plane which bisects the body about waist level; the Door Plane, which divides the space forward of the body from the space behind; and the Wheel which separates the right side of the body from the left.

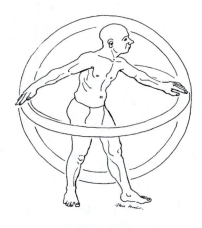

Table Plane

Wheel Plane

Door Plane

Fig. 5. The planes of shape.

The three planes are more usually referred to as **Horizontal, Vertical** and **Sagittal**. Movement in each of them can vary anywhere between two extremes:

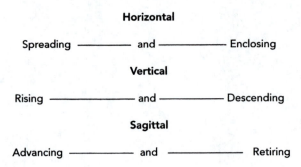

Horizontal

Spreading ————— and ————— Enclosing

Vertical

Rising ————— and ————— Descending

Sagittal

Advancing ————— and ————— Retiring

1. In the Horizontal plane movement can be Spreading to open and reveal the body and reach the furthest rim of one's kinesphere. This would be an expansive, opening movement, whilst the opposite of Enclosing is gathering oneself together, shaping the body as if to close oneself off from the outside world.

2. In the Vertical plane the possibilities are Rising led by the upper body and possibly curving sideways, and Descending, which can also be a sideways curving through the body and waist. The Shape in this plane is best imagined as being between two planes of glass.

3. Sagittal movements on the other hand involve leaning forward with the torso to make a convex shape, or bending the torso backwards to make a concave, retiring movement.

This Sagittal convex and concave movement is in the forwards and backwards directions and is quite different in appearance from the opening and closing shaping of the horizontal plane. Movement along the Vertical plane is one of display, "Here I am!" with no closing or retreating quality. It is possible of course, for a movement to contain more than one of these directions – to be enclosing and retiring, or rising and advancing for example.

Think of the movements of colleagues or friends and it is easy to see that different people favour different ways to Shape their movement. It is also immediately apparent that the way they do so goes a long way to determining what impression they give to others. One person will curl himself up the moment he gets into conversation and almost look as if he is peering out of a tunnel at the world, another will put her head up and her shoulders back as if to make herself look important. And yet another will turn this way and that vaguely as if they were paying no attention at all.

These then were the planes in which Laban saw movement being shaped, the architectural quality of movement, but his primary concern after arriving in Britain was to explore Eukinetics, the Effort content of movement.

THREE QUALITIES OF MOVEMENT — EFFORT

As with Shape there are three types of Effort, but these are qualities rather than directions of movement. If a movement has, say an Enclosing Shape, it will also probably have some quality of Effort, and in this case it may give that Enclosing action the nature of, say, a quick hug. How then would one describe the Effort content of that movement?

Laban identified the three qualities of Effort as **Space**, **Weight** and **Time**, and like the three planes of Shape they each have their contrasting polarities between which they vary:

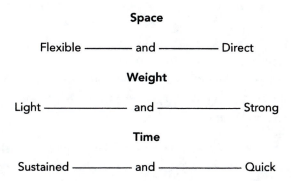

Space

Flexible ———— and ———— Direct

Weight

Light ———————— and ———————— Strong

Time

Sustained ———— and ———— Quick

1. Space is the total space of one's kinesphere, the full extent of the 'bubble' in which we move. Space Effort is then the quality of movement we use to explore our kinesphere. This can be done in a flexible, general way, or in an investigative, direct way.

2. Weight is the type of pressure put into an action. It can either be a diminishing pressure with the appearance of lightness and delicacy, or it can be an increasing, assertive pressure. In a hug it would be the latter.

3. Time is the pace contained in movement, either speeding it up or slowing it down and would be another quality contained in a quick hug.

From this we can say therefore that if an Enclosing action takes the form of an embrace, it is likely that the Effort content that movement will contain will be either Weight [probably Increasing Pressure] or Time [either Sustained or Quick] and it will be the nature of the Effort which determines whether this is a hug or an embrace. Neither Effort nor Shape can go on indefinitely; the person being hugged will have to be released! To arrive at a polarity would be to make further movement impossible, the movement has to be reversed to avoid some sort of paralysis. Effort and Shape are therefore constantly fluctuating somewhere along their continuums. One person will use Space Effort more on the investigative side, another more on the exploring end of the continuum. Yet another person will have very little if any activity of this nature, but more in the Weight range and so on.

Shape and Effort are therefore concerned with the direction and quality of movement, they do not describe fixed positions. Everyone makes a different combination of both Shape and Effort in the three ranges. It is worth experimenting with some elementary movements of each quality of Effort to get the feel of it.

1. Space – let the arm move loosely around the body in any plane and imagine what one might be doing. The hand perhaps followed by the eye is exploring the environment – 'having a look around' the room or the landscape or whatever, taking in everything in a loose, sweeping, way. Try then to make this more specific by pointing a finger very precisely at something. The movement then becomes much more investigative. Movement of this type we therefore associate with a range between exploring and investigating, according to how flexible or direct it is in quality.

2. Weight – this is concerned with how heavy or light we make an action, for example bringing one's hand down in a forceful way, or doing so with a lightness of touch, and how we vary the pressure between the two. To give a movement weight qualities therefore requires different degrees of pressure ranging between "putting the pressure on" and lightly diminishing pressure.

3. Time – imagine a runner ready for the "off" on the starting blocks, then springing forward into action. The whole focus of the athlete's movement has to be exercising some degree of timing towards a defined end, in this case at the fastest possible speed. He is going to "go for it" and his speed will perhaps increase as he runs. As he hits the tape he will then decelerate to a gradual stop. This then is the range of timing of movement, and we do it equally with an arm or a leg as we do with the whole body. In enclosing a per-

son we can make this action a quick hug, or we can make it a slow embrace. Either way it will contain elements of both speeding up and slowing down of the arms and other parts of the body involved in the action at various times.

LABAN'S EIGHT BASIC EFFORTS

The six Effort Components were transposed onto the diagram as shown in Fig. 6. Laban then identified the eight most common Effort movements, and his Effort script for each of them is taken directly from the Effort Diagram.

If the 6 Effort Components are:-

SPACE	(a) Flexible	(b) Direct
WEIGHT	(c) Light	(d) Strong
TIME	(e) Sustained	(f) Quick

then various combinations of these produce the notation for each of the 8 Basic Efforts as:

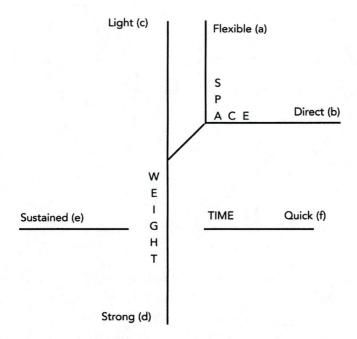

Fig. 6   The Effort Diagram which forms the basis for symbols used in Effort notation

[a] + [c] + [e]	Floating	
[b] + [d] + [f]	Punching	
[b] + [c] + [e]	Gliding	
[a] + [d] + [f]	Slashing	
[b] + [c] + [f]	Dabbing	
[a] + [d] + [e]	Wringing	
[a] + [c] + [f]	Flicking	
[b] + [d] + [e]	Pressing	

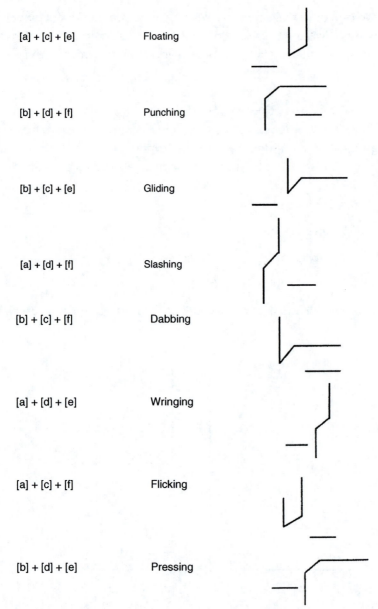

"These can be considered basically like eight notes of music, which may be composed in an unlimited number of ways. It is the composition of the efforts which is expressive; everyone is normally capable of using them all." Warren Lamb, *Dance Magazine*, January 1952, in the article for which the Andy Warhol sketches were commissioned.

This then was the basis of the system of Effort notation used by Warren Lamb when he set out to do his first industrial observations in 1948. In describing procedures in a factory it might be used alongside linear motif writing as shown for example in the Mars notations, but notation of Effort was all Warren Lamb required as his work increasingly involved interviewing managers. The notations would be made during a two hour interview after which the number of occurrences of each effort sign was calculated. The significance of the result in terms of ability or inclination to any particular type of work could then be analysed.

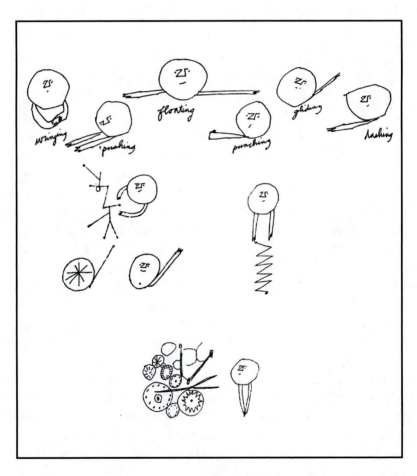

In 1962 *Dance Magazine* commissioned a young, relatively unknown artist called Andy Warhol to illustrate an article on movement analysis by Warren Lamb, with sketches of Laban's 8 Basic Efforts

A recurring problem throughout his career has been to find suitable terminology to describe observations. Just as Kinetography had to be adapted from dance to work situations, so the terminology had also to be fine-tuned. The result of this has been to change the terms for the polarities of Effort to ones more related to work behaviour:

Indirecting [Flexible] ————————————— Directing [Direct]

Diminishing pressure [Light] ————— Increasing pressure [Strong]

Decelerating [Sustained] ————————— Accelerating [Quick]

THE IMPORTANCE OF FLOW

Another important quality of movement was identified by Laban and given further definition by Warren Lamb. This is the Flow element. The concept of Flow in movement is most easily explained by imagining the movements of an infant before any social interaction has required it to discipline its movements. Gradually as a person grows up the movement becomes controlled and the element of Flow diminishes. For a person brought up in a highly sophisticated and ritualised society the element of Flow left in their movement at adulthood may be small. Where the perception of perfection is obeying a series of rules and every gesture has significance, Flow is ironed out of behaviour. At the other extreme, where there are few social pressures – where children are allowed to grow up 'wild' – there is likely to be much more Flow in the adult behaviour. Warren Lamb describes this condition of movement as 'childlike' which is quite separate from the less desirable quality of 'childish'.

Flow is a dynamic of movement, giving it flexibility and grace, and allowing for originality. It easily links whole body movements and gestures, and gives balance. Effort, whether Space, Weight or Time, flows in the sense of being more free or more controlled. If you allow yourself to be blown along by the wind so that your legs go faster and faster, then you resist the wind and control your running, you have gone from **Freeing** to **Binding** Flow. Some people vary the Flow of Effort a lot, going almost from one extreme to the other, whilst others use very little variation at all, giving all their movements a sameness, a lack of variety. Flow of Effort can therefore be plotted on its continuum:

FLOW OF EFFORT

Freeing ——————————————————————— Binding

A girl blown by the wind.

Similarly Flow of Shape operates on a continuum, this time between **Growing** and **Shrinking**. This has to do with our use of the "space bubble" or Kinesphere which we carry around ourselves. Some people like to vary its size between big, even beyond their physical reach, down to a small shrunk Kinesphere. Others will operate more in one than the other with very little variation. It is very easy to imagine the difference in impact between a person who operates on the Growing side of the continuum to the person on the Shrinking side, and it has nothing to do with their physical size. Many very large people will constantly try to make themselves smaller, and conversely small people regularly operate at the furthest extreme of their Kinesphere.

The concept of Flow of Shape was first described by Warren Lamb and its continuum looks like this:

FLOW OF SHAPE

Growing ———————————————————————————— Shrinking

A simple example from Warren Lamb's records will demonstrate the effectiveness of Growing in Flow of Shape. A General Manager of a subsidiary company, Mr A, commented that he greatly respected his Group Chief Executive Mr X, for his handling of a group of people. "When Mr X is talking to a group," said Mr A, "I have observed him to take a step or two backwards to preserve a distance between himself and the group and this seems to set him apart as a leader. However, when I try to do the same thing people follow me!" Actually Mr X was Growing as he stepped back, giving himself a bigger kinesphere and thus maintaining the same contact with his audience who felt no need to close a gap. Mr A did not have the capacity to Grow his kinesphere, and his group tried to follow him to maintain contact.

The way in which we use Flow therefore has a critical impact on the effectiveness of the Shape and Effort in our movement. A Directing Effort combined with Binding Flow is quite different in appearance to one combined with Freeing Flow, an altogether gentler action. Similarly a Descending movement combined with its affinity of Increasing Pressure seems emphatic, but where it is combined with Freeing Flow as opposed to Binding Flow it will lose its power. It will be a slap rather than a punch, a point that will become more significant when gender is considered.

The basis for the notation learnt by Warren Lamb at the Art of Movement Studio was contained in the ideas of Effort and Flow. Shape was not at that time included in such observations. When Warren Lamb began working in industry he was in his own perception still a dance student who in a short time had learnt a lot about movement and a little about Effort notation. For some time he continued to put dance first, though it was often subsidised by his work for Paton, Lawrence & Co. Gradually his artistic life was superseded by the need to earn, and to that end he developed methods of analysis and notation so that they could be extensively applied in the more lucrative fields of executive selection and career development.

Of all the people connected with Laban in Britain, only Lawrence and Lamb made any contribution in industry and only Lamb in the area of interpretation of movement. Lawrence never put his work onto a permanent footing, so the field was wide open for Lamb when he arrived on the scene. Whether Laban would altogether approve of his having taken movement study so far into the managerial field he sometimes doubts. Laban's dream always remained the resurgence of movement choirs bringing thousands of workers together for soul-uplifting movement and dance experience, restoring their sense of their individual dignity.

But Warren Lamb was and still is faithful to the overall purpose behind Laban's crusade – that of recognising movement as the common denominator to all human activity, whether in work, social or spiritual life. At the same time he remembered the paramount importance of individuality and its expression through movement.

CHAPTER FOUR

ARRIVING AT APTITUDE ASSESSMENT

WORKING ON THE FACTORY FLOOR

S oon after joining the Art of Movement Studio Warren Lamb had to think of ways of subsidising his dance training once his war service gratuity ran out. The most rewarding employment he found was posing for Manchester art clubs, three of which employed him regularly. He tried out unusual poses and felt honour bound to hold them as still as possible, in spite of the resulting aches and pains, and despite the fact that he was urged to be less conscientious.

Laban and Lawrence already had every confidence in Lamb's notation ability and suggested he should help them with their work for Paton Lawrence and Co. After some demurring about the affect this would have on his dance training, Lamb agreed to a salary of £4 a week for which he would provide observations as required under Laban's supervision. The accountants and engineers at Paton, Lawrence and Co. thought "the old man has gone off his rocker" when they saw the rather off-beat dancer Lawrence wanted them to present to their clients.

Daniel Ellis was one of the consultants at Paton Lawrence and Co. He was an industrial engineer brought up on stop-watch studies, who worked aggressively to improve productivity for his clients, and drove himself to a fatal heart-attack in his early 40s. Ellis was outspoken in his scepticism of everything to do with Laban. He openly described Lawrence as being "round the bend" in attempting to introduce Laban's work into industry but he was loyal and complied when Lawrence stood his ground.

One of Lamb's first assignments was with Broadhead & Graves, a manufacturer of fine worsted material in Huddersfield. As Ellis's car struggled over the Pennines from Manchester he barked questions at Lamb about this "movement stuff" and how was it supposed to help the client. With so little experience behind him, all of it irrelevant to weaving, Lamb must have been hard-pushed to find convincing answers.

On arrival he dived into the weaving shed and began making notations of the workers using Laban's Effort Graphs. Every now and then Ellis pounced to see what he was up to and demanded to know what this or that worker had been doing when a particular notation was made. Lamb also quizzed Ellis on the types of movement necessary, the degree of pressure required, the need for speed or not. Together they worked out detailed job specifications in movement terms for all the tasks, and these were then related to his observations of the workers.

Their movements were still classified according to Laban's categories of Functional, Shadow and Body Attitude, but already Lamb found it necessary to adapt Laban's 8 Basic Efforts, which were too general for the precision required in making industrial observations. There was just enough that was scientific about Lamb's observations to appeal to Ellis, and in the end he was won over by their accuracy. They disagreed on the Motion Study principle, of course, and Ellis was eventually persuaded of the need to take into account the individuality of the operatives.

It was also at Broadhead & Graves where Ellis was putting in a new costing system that the first opportunity arose to use movement observation for a purely managerial post, when Ellis enlisted Lamb's help in advising on the suitability of a particular candidate they had in mind for the position of office manager. The theory that a person's aptitudes can be discovered from analysis of their movement pattern was about to be tested.

The nature of the manager's job was studied and between 40 and 50 features of it were listed in movement terms based on the 6 Effort Components. Lamb then used movement observations taken entirely in an interview to work out how far the movement profile of the candidate matched the job specification he had drawn up. What significance did this have for the way he would perform the job, and how would he be perceived by his colleagues to be performing the job?

He gave his assessment of the candidate to Ellis, describing how the man's natural way of working fitted against the specifications, and ending his assessment with a summary of his strengths and weaknesses for the position. The observations taken by Lamb of the candidate in that one interview turned out to be identical to those already made of him by Ellis over several days. Ellis was impressed, and after this always relied on Lamb for key appointments. He became a great supporter and advocate of Laban. He asked to play a part in the foundation of the Laban Guild, the only British institution to which Laban gave his name and which still thrives today in setting a lead for recreational dance. He also offered his services as administrator to a number of Laban activities and his early death was a great loss. The pattern used at Broadhead & Graves was repeated in other companies, and job specifications worked out in movement terms were of a similar length of 40 to 50 items. In later years this would be reduced to 15 to 20.

The Glaxo Company at Barnard Castle was another company in which Ellis and Lamb worked together. There some 300 women performed about 25 different operations in the filling and packaging department. Many of the operations were highly repetitive, one person doing nothing more than press caps on vials of penicillin as they went by. Warren Lamb made observations of all 300 workers and specifications of each operation. On the basis of matching one with the other, they moved the majority of the women to different jobs. This was done overnight, and naturally met with some resistance. After they had settled down however, productivity increased by over 30% and was maintained. The moves were supported by recommendations on both the training and choice of supervisors, again based on Lamb's assessments.

Lamb was also involved in many managerial appointments at Glaxo. Where candidates were already in post advice would be given on how their potential could be maximized and what arrangements could be made to compensate for their shortcomings.

It was a logical step, still in the early fifties, to move into operative team-building. At Faithful Overalls, now Faithful Ltd, another Paton, Lawrence & Co client, Lamb worked on an assignment which involved this time about 200 women. In this instance each woman worked on one part of the overalls and they were later assembled into the whole garment. Some sewed on a pocket, others the buttons, others stitched a collar, and so on. Lamb studied all the operations, actually working on some of the sewing machines himself, to the amusement of the ladies. And of course he recorded the movements of all 200. On this occasion, together with another colleague from Paton, Lawrence & Co called Reg Carslake, he used his findings to reorganise the women into teams of twenty. Each team had responsibility for making a whole garment and each person had to be skilled in at least two operations. He also advised on the person most suited to be the team leader. Carslake made some innovations to the layout of the bench and the installation of aids like gravity shutes for passing work on to another member of the team. This was not quite an overnight switch because it had to be done in sections, but it created all the more problems of resistance to change. Eventually it was completed, however, and proved to be highly successful. Not only was productivity higher but the workers, almost without exception, said how much they liked being in a team. A similar system known as quality circles was used in Japan and USA in later years, but no doubt with different methods for choosing the groups and their leaders.

Whilst Laban and Lamb after him had the genius to develop this method of assessing people in a work situation, the unsung hero is the far-sighted F.C. Lawrence who saw the potential and created the opportunity for their talents to be put to use. He went on to set up one of the first management schools in Britain.

Women working for Faithful Overalls, now Faithfull Ltd, 1955

Unfortunately his work was not marketed, organised or supported by adequate finance and PR. He and those around him were much better at ensuring the success of their clients than at promoting themselves. Later when marketing had become an important industry in its own right, it may have been a different story.

THE LABAN LAWRENCE EFFORT ASSESSMENT

By 1950 a substantial number of clients were asking for Lamb's assessments, and Lawrence's colleagues were impressed and delighted with his success. The Laban-Lawrence Effort Assessment was developed and offered as a selection tool and also proved popular. This was not a fixed test given in the same form to everyone. It was the procedure already used by Laban and Lamb of analyzing a managerial position in movement terms, observing the candidate and producing a report on his or her Strengths, Weaknesses and Development Possibilities. In other words it was a new label for the same 'system'. It had not been scientifically tested, but nevertheless more and more people placed confidence in it. [See Appendix II]

This was a time of burgeoning research and experiment into personality tests. Some had been developed during World War II and were now adapted for use in industry by institutions such as The National Institute of Industrial Psychology and the Tavistock Institute. The Catell 16PF [Personality Factors] was a favourite.

The problem with any such form of assessment is that it depends to some degree on self-perception. The subject answers a set of questions which it is claimed has been so cleverly devised that subjectivity is excluded from the result. Still today almost every test or interview technique relies on people answering questions about themselves. Graphology and astrology can be counted as exceptions. But even in the 1950s there were some voicing concern that a person could be trained to do well at tests and interviews. The promoters claim that the tests eliminate the possibility of faking the result, but are they always a step ahead of the "cheaters"? Even intelligence testing is vulnerable in this respect, and gives limited information on the candidate.

In 1982 James Flynn put forward the surprise results of his research – since known as the Flynn Effect – that if IQ tests were to be believed, people had become progressively more intelligent since the beginning of the century to 1950. After that IQ levels stood still but problem-solving ability improved at an even greater rate. The findings, if correct, obviously make a nonsense of IQ testing, but even though there are many who believe such tests are iniquitous, racist and aim to preserve a ruling elite they are still a popular method of selection.

The 16PF questionnaire has now passed its 50th birthday and is still in use as a recruitment tool by a wide variety of organisations. It is seen as a quick and easy method of arriving at a short list of candidates who are asked to answer as frankly as possible a range of questions about themselves, thus revealing a "behavioural profile". No doubt this is one step ahead of an unskilled interview, but apart from the difficulty of devising a test which is free from cultural bias and "cheat-proof", is such deep and personal interrogation of strangers acceptable?

Certainly we are obsessed with methods of analysing and categorising ourselves. The tabloids regularly carry features inviting us to find out more about ourselves. By answering multi-choice questions you will discover how good is your marriage, how healthily you eat, how passionate/fit/economic you are. In the end the most revelatory aspect of all these tests is the degree to which people love to analyse and categorise themselves.

Tests of ability as opposed to behaviour are first encountered at school, and now children are tested more than ever before, strangely enough more to find out if their teachers are performing than anything else. Sadly education systems have progressively narrowed their values to that which can be easily measured, and now reward academic achievement to the exclusion of almost any other form of attainment. Schools which once prided themselves on the quality of person they produced are now more concerned to be high on the exam league tables. The sad result has been both to devalue degrees and to condemn to a sense of failure many talented people because they did not jump through the pseudo-academic hoops at the required time. The prospects for Western Civilisation are frightening if the people rewarded with power are those highly skilled at passing examinations and scoring in tests, abilities which could probably be programmed into a computer. The need for a more reliable method of assessment and selection has never been greater.

Other qualities of character and aptitude have to be set alongside measurable qualifications to give the whole picture of the value of an individual to a potential employer. In assessment by movement observation there are no failures, although certainly some may prove to have a much wider range of abilities than others. The objective is to discover and describe the individual's preferred way of operating both physically and mentally. There is no 'ideal' against which that person is measured. An assessment can be made either at a given task or, as had already become the accepted in the early 1950s, in an interview situation.

In the interview the candidate can give whatever answers he or she chooses, true or false, and the subject can be whatever they care to discuss. The interview could even be conducted in a language the observer did not understand. None of what is said will impact on the pattern of movement emerging during the interview. Even if the candidate knew what movement to simulate to create a particular effect [which is highly unlikely except in the crudest terms] it is impossible, according to Lamb, for someone to maintain a 'fake' for any length of time. In fact evidence of inconsistency in a person's movement pattern would in itself have a significance, and the reason for the 'cover up' would be of interest. Lamb's later study of Posture-Gesture-Mergers is important in this respect.

The information gained from a movement study of a candidate is therefore quite different in its value from that obtained from a person's perception of themselves, and would be complementary to all other information. At the same time it has the enormous advantage of being non-intrusive. There is no need to drive a candidate by perhaps impertinent and upsetting questioning to bare their soul and reveal their anxieties. Their true strengths and weaknesses will be evident from their movement without the reason for them being discussed. Qualifica-

Warren Lamb (right) making notations while Ellis (left) talks to a client

tions and work experience can be checked quite easily and put alongside the final assessment to give a complete picture of the individual's potential.

This freedom from self-assessment was the unique selling point of The Laban Lawrence Personal Assessment. At this time Lamb's priority was still to dance with the British Dance Theatre, but 'resting' periods allowed him ample time for assessment work, and he was forever travelling from London to Lancashire and Yorkshire where most of his clients were.

Occasionally he invited Ellis to watch him dance. Ellis wrote to Laban in December 1950, enclosing some of Lamb's assessments for Glaxo: "Last Tuesday I was privileged to see the British Dance Theatre and it will probably amuse you to know that, at long last, I am beginning to appreciate the meaning and form of most of their work. Certainly the group has developed tremendously since I was last privileged to see them at Stretford Town Hall, particularly Miss Preston [Valerie Preston Dunlop], whose vitality of expression is most notable."

Photograph: Warren Lamb writing notation

As the volume of work increased, there were enthusiastic plans for training more people who could make movement observations, a plan which probably mercifully, did not materialise. The idea had been that the observers would then send their graphs to Warren Lamb for him to interpret, but there must have been some concern with the validity of observations made by people quickly trained. As it was Warren Lamb did not relish the thought of being stuck at a desk interpreting other people's assessments.

In 1952 Laban and Lawrence changed the name of their system from Personal Effort Assessment to the Laban Lawrence Test, on the grounds that this would be much easier to sell. Lamb knew nothing of it till he saw the printed stationery and he was indignant. He pointed out that the uniqueness of their system was that it was not a 'test' people could pass or fail, but an assessment of their aptitudes in relation to a particular job specification. There was always the likelihood that a person who did not match up for one particular job might prove highly suitable for another. It was Laban who had taught Lamb to value the over-riding uniqueness of the individual, and now, he argued, here he was allowing his analysis to be called a test at which by implication a person could fail. The argument in Lamb's view was to protect the purity of their method of assessment against commercial pragmatism. It was an argument he would have to fight on other occasions during his career. It led to his departure from Action Profilers International at a much later date.

The Laban Lawrence test was in fact no different from the previously called Assessment [as Appendix II shows], but the outcome of the argument was Lamb's declaration of independence in 1952. He continued to do some work for Laban and Lawrence, but in future operated primarily under the name of Warren Lamb Associates. The separation was amicable and gradually the Laban Lawrence Test fell into disuse as Warren Lamb developed and used his own method of movement analysis, Aptitude Assessment.

APTITUDE ASSESSMENT

The dictionary definition he found for 'Aptitude' as a 'natural ability, disposition, tendency, fitness, suitableness' seemed appropriate for the diagnosis he was making. He was not measuring ability, but describing the way in which a candidate preferred to work. A range of options was then possible.

- He could offer individual career guidance by identifying the types of work most congenial to someone with those aptitudes;

- He could weigh their suitability for a particular job as part of a selection process;

- He could advise on how the individual would perform in a team and what qualities would be desirable in other team members to enhance his strengths or compensate for his weaknesses.

These were the three lines of assessment offered by the newly formed Warren Lamb Associates.

Lamb still spent many evenings poring over Effort Observations with Laban, matching candidates to job specifications by dividing their qualities into Strengths, Development Possibilities and Inert [which he later changed to Weaknesses]. The categories related to the degree to which the individual kept movement alive relative to each item in the Effort Graph. If there was any movement in a range, say between Indirecting and Directing, even if this tended towards paralysis at an extreme end of the range, this merited "Development Possibility", in that where some movement in the range existed, the person could be helped to move their range of Effort away from the extreme.

The process compares with adding vocabulary to a foreign language when a person already has a grasp of the basic grammar of that language to build on. Where a neutralising or a locking component resulted in an absence of movement in one range, then this area would be described as a Weakness since where no movement existed there was no 'language' to build on. But where there was easy fluid movement in a particular range there was life – or Strength. This was the theory on which he successfully based his Aptitude Assessment, and which later also formed the basis of the Action Profilers Framework.

THE 3-STAGE DECISION-MAKING PROCESS

The most significant development in forming the Aptitude Assessment however, was the identification of the three stages of the Effort Graph as the logical stages in a Decision-Making Process. Laban had not understood the concept of a Decision-Making Process. Although he had referred to relating Space Effort to Attention, of Weight to Intention, of Time to Decision, he never referred to these as parts of a process. This was probably because he was first and foremost a dancer and choreographer and his interest had been primarily to identify qualities to help actors and in particular dance mime. It was Warren Lamb who saw the three qualities as a logical progression, as a pattern of movement each person would have to follow in their own particular way throughout their waking lives.

The premise is that the progression from the initial formulation of an idea to its fruition in an action consists of three stages:

ATTENTION

Indirecting ———————— SPACE ———————— Directing

INTENTION

Diminishing Pressure ——— WEIGHT ——— Increasing Pressure

COMMITMENT

Decelerating ———————— TIME ———————— Accelerating

Stage One - ATTENTION: [Space] A situation must first be given attention. How this attention is given can vary between being very general and unparticular to being very detailed according to how we are inclined to collect information on the matter before proceeding to the next stage. It may also of course be given in one way then the other. The physical appearance of the possible range of Attention varies between a very casual looking around, to the other extreme of scrutinizing closely.

Stage Two - INTENTION: [Weight] Having assembled whatever amount of information we want, we then have to decide on the 'weightiness' of the matter to us. Do we regard this as a matter of importance, and if so what stance should we take? Do we approve or disapprove; do we care or not care? Does the matter need to be treated with authority or delicacy, with Diminishing Pressure or Increasing Pressure?

Stage Three - COMMITMENT: [Time] On the basis of what we have found out [stage one] and what we have decided is our opinion on the matter [stage two], we must then decide to act – or not, and if we do, when to do so. Laban had called this stage Decision, but Lamb changed it to Commitment in that it is the point at which we make a commitment to action. Some people are constantly 'leaping into action', others will constantly avoid doing anything; most people live somewhere between the two extremes.

All our activity is a series of Decision-Making Processes ranging from the infinitesimally small to those great enough to change the course of our lives. Everyone has their own way of arriving at a decision, and according to Warren Lamb it is naturally and constantly demonstrated by our movement pattern which relates physically to the mental processes involved. The pattern emerging is totally individual and this is what is revealed by careful notation of a person's movements simply sitting in a chair and chatting for a couple of hours. Decision-taking is a substantial part of life, and especially of business life where the quality of decision-taking will have the most direct bearing on profitability. To be able to predict for an employer how a particular person would behave in a given situation was to provide information more valuable than any test coloured by subjectivity could offer. It would also reveal how usefully or otherwise a person with all the necessary qualifications on paper would actually perform – their Action Quotient.

To the movement analyst it is not significant how we sit or stand, but how we go from one position to another. How much Effort we expend moving in each of these planes determines our disposition to particular types of occupation and relationships. An explanation of how this movement pattern is established in the individual is the subject of Chapter Six.

To give some elementary examples, a person who showed little spatial activity in either directing or indirecting their Attention would hardly be suited to original research; they would not know where to look and would have little inclination to do so. They would even find it stressful to have to try to perform in this way for long. A person who was strong in Intention and full of authoritative attitudes would hardly make a caring nurse or counsellor, but they might be good at work involving organising priorities or seeing that rules are obeyed.

People do not simply react to circumstances. They react so as to be able to take action in a preferred way that is in accordance with their character, so long as they are free to do so. No two people react in exactly the same way. On the other hand we are often not free to follow our preference as much as we would like; conditions are so dominating that we are compelled to act in a prescribed way whether it is in line with our preference or not. If this happens a lot and we can seldom use our preferred way of behaviour, we will start to behave unnaturally like a puppet and suffer some form of stress, whatever the work, however senior or lowly. In reality wherever possible people will mould their jobs to suit their preferred way of working, so no two people have the same impact in a given position; the job/person relationship is a two-way process. There are many different ways, for example, of exercising leadership, just as there are as many different ways of selling. When a director of a company or a new head-teacher is appointed a change will take place in the whole ethos of the department or the school, because the impact of any two people on a work force will be quite different.

The subtleties and varieties of individual movement patterns cannot be exaggerated. They are as varied as people themselves. Even identical twins will have different movement patterns reflecting their different dispositions. To this has to be added the degree of Flow contained in their movement. Whether it is Free or Bound, or contains very little Flow, will determine the amount of dynamism in a person's actions and therefore how their aptitudes are used. It is extremely complex and only a trained observer can truly identify the tell-tale phrases of movement which recur several times over a short period and indicate a person's aptitudes and personality.

ADDING SHAPE TO THE FORMULA

Laban's preference for treating Choreutics and Eukinetics – Shape and Effort – separately when he was teaching has already been referred to. In his industrial work when he arrived in Britain, as has also been explained he was primarily concerned with analysing Eukinetics or Effort. He regarded this as relevant to work, while the Shape of a person's movement related to their spiritual and mystical selves. To Warren Lamb this was not so easy. He increasingly found that to arrive at the deeper understanding of the individual which it was now apparent movement study could provide, it was necessary to take Shape and Effort equally into account. Since Laban had never used Effort and Shape together, neither had Lamb to this point. It was not until 1957, the year before Laban died, that Lamb eventually asked him if there was any reason why Shape should not be included in movement analysis. Laban seemed surprised as Lamb made out his case for looking at the two together. In the type of analysis he was now doing – as opposed to the largely operative work originally studied by Laban – a more rounded picture of the candidate could be achieved by adding Shape observations to the notations. Laban agreed, but he was tired and the discussion went no further. Immediately Lamb began work on matching Effort and Shape, and to his observation of Shape he also added the significant notion of the Flow of Shape between Growing and Shrinking.

The three aspects of Shape and Effort were described in the previous chapter. The qualities on the left of the Effort ranges can be described as Indulging and those on the right as Contending. In the Shape ranges those on the left can be described as Convex and those on the right as Concave.

Indulging	EFFORT	Contending
Indirecting ————————	[Space]	———————— Directing
Diminishing Pressure ————	[Weight]	————Increasing Pressure
Decelerating ———————	[Time]	——————— Accelerating
Freeing ————————	FLOW	———————— Binding

Convex	SHAPE	Concave
Spreading ———————	[Horizontal]	———————Enclosing
Rising —————————	[Vertical]	——————— Descending
Advancing ———————	[Sagittal]	——————— Retiring
Growing ————————	FLOW	——————— Shrinking

In adding an analysis of Shape to his Aptitude Assessment, Warren Lamb was eager to discover the degree to which there was an affinity in a person's movement between their Shape and Effort, and to establish the significance of this. In the Horizontal Plane, for example, it is natural for a Convex Spreading movement to have an Indulging Indirecting quality and for a Concave Enclosing movement to have a Contending Directing Effort. In the Vertical Plane a similar affinity is between Rising and Diminishing Pressure and Descending and Increasing Pressure. It is much easier to exert pressure with a downward than an upward action. In the Sagittal Plane the affinity is between Advancing and Deceleration – a measured unrushed approach – and Retiring and Acceleration, suggesting a strategic or nervous pulling away from something. The opposites are of course possible as in the case of "Fools rush in!" The qualities of Flow have similar affinities.

Warren Lamb was now concerned to examine the occurrence or otherwise of these affinities between Shape and Effort in a person's movement and to assess the significance of the degree of correlation. If a person did not make the natural combination, what was the reason for this and what was the impact upon the personality?

Imagine a politician making a speech. If he tries to emphasise a point by bringing his hand and arm down he will probably also bring his head and shoulders down in a descending way, his Effort of emphasizing will be matched by his Shape. The affinity of the two will give extra emphasis to his speech. To bring his hand down but to rise with his body would give a very different impression, more suited to announcing a known fact than making a key point in an argument. In this example the Effort and Shape have affinity therefore, in that the Effort contained in the movement is one of [Contending] Increasing Pressure, and the Shape is in the [Concave] Descending aspect of the Vertical plane. The impression is one of harmony. Where a person's behaviour lacks these affinities, if the speaker thumps the table without any Concave Shaping in the Vertical plane, but perhaps more in a Convex and even Advancing Shape, the observer may feel that something is not at all right. The behaviour will seem uncoordinated or even contrived, and the observer may feel they can't trust in the sincerity of what the speaker is saying.

Combining observations of Shape and Effort in his assessments was highly significant in Warren Lamb's development of movement observation. In notation terms he used the same techniques as he used for notating Effort, but with a double tail on the end of each vertical to indicate Shape.

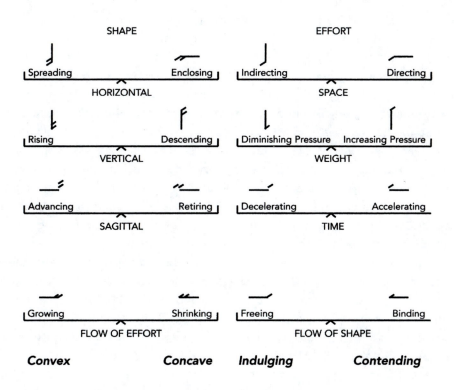

Fig. 7. Summary of Shape and Effort Variations with their notations.

POSTURE AND GESTURE

The way had now been opened for a further and highly significant development. It was the realisation by Warren Lamb that what had been previously recorded as Functional, Shadow and Body Attitude could more realistically be regarded as only two categories which he saw as Posture and Gesture. Again this was a distinction which Laban as a choreographer would not have arrived at, but was of importance where movement study was used as a method of analysis. The definitions he gave to each were:

POSTURE: an action involving continuous adjustment of every part of the body, with consistency in the process of variation [comparable with Laban's Body Attitude].

GESTURE: an action confined to a part or parts of the body, which very often would be functional [a combination of Laban's definition of Functional and Shadow Movement].

Having identified these as the basic elements of individual movement, he then studied the relationship of one to the other. Did a gesture appear out of a postural adjustment, or did it perhaps precede and merge into a postural adjustment? Did a gesture perhaps remain only a gesture, with no further significance? Imagine a man saying something like "I would like to bring everyone together to solve this thing rationally." He might raise his arms to encompass an imaginary group and as he does so merge this action into a postural adjustment by also lifting his torso. In this case the gesture has merged into the posture. If the action remained a gesture with no postural adjustment the speaker would be so much less convincing.

What Warren Lamb found was that in everyone's behaviour there is a point at which the two merge, and that this merger takes place repeatedly. The manner of the merger of Posture and Gesture in a person's movement – their PGM – is the essential DNA of their behaviour. It is unique to the individual. In making movement observations ever since, this Posture Gesture Merger is the core behaviour which has to be identified, that which distinguishes one person from every other.

If all parts of the body are transcribing the same shape, this is Posture. If only a part of the body is "performing" – a hand and arm, or the head, then this is Gesture. A person will in their normal behaviour integrate their gestures with their whole body movement, and they will do so several times during the course of an interview. In fact they would find it extremely difficult not to do so.

A person trying to give a contrived impression will have to make body adjustments during pauses in the conversation, or while the interviewer is speaking. In the meantime he or she may make a series of gestures without any adjustment to their posture. This may not be deliberate lying, although there have been occasions when Warren Lamb has been able to identify the person in a team either causing trouble or actually stealing by this understanding of their movement patterns. It could of course simply be an over-anxious desire to please or nervousness, but a heightened anxiety for whatever reason will manifest itself in a lack of merger between Posture and Gesture and this in itself is significant. It is a warning signal to the interviewer. The interviewee, on the other hand, if asked how he felt during the interview, might say "uncomfortable".

The significance of the identification of PGM, or Integrated Movement as it is also sometimes called, cannot be over-emphasised. It emerges in an individual's behaviour during adolescence, and usually by the age of twenty would be more or less established for life. Only trauma will substantially alter a person's PGM.

We all, of course, are liable to adopt fashionable mannerisms which will be with us for a few months or years before they are dropped. Women often adjust their movements to suit the height of their heels and the length or width of hemlines, and for many years girls with long hair had a prescribed way of throwing it back from their faces – a mannerism which some would perform by the minute.

Social mores may also affect the degree to which some actions remain as gestures or become merged behaviour. A greeting, for example, can be with or without merging. If you are introduced to someone at a cocktail party or at a business lunch you expect to shake hands and smile your "How-do-you-does". It can be a handshake pure and simple, a Gesture, and that is the only behaviour you expect from someone you may never see again. It is socially permissible for a subtle, controlled merging to take place; as the hand comes forward [Directing] the other arm may come round to lightly touch your arm [Enclosing]. This is something practiced by many politicians and for which Bill Clinton as president was particularly noted. The Enclosing may not even be to touch, but simply to shape the body in such a way as to make you feel this person is giving you their full attention, which is probably the warmest and most flattering degree of embrace. The more the stranger you are meeting merges his Posture and Gesture at this point, the greater the impact he or she will probably have. If you see that person again you may remember them.

If on the other hand he or she pretends a tremendous enthusiasm you will probably smell a rat or feel embarrassed and make a mental note to give them a wide berth in future. To shake hands lightly without eye contact and with no postural adjustment is no more than a meaningless social ritual but that is very often all that is required or expected. In our over-civilised and sophisticated social mores, to go in "feet first" and enthusiastically shake the other person up and down is definitely not acceptable.

An enthusiastic handshake

An embrace between old friends, or between lovers greeting each other need have no such restraints. Affinities of Effort and Shape are expected. There are no bounds to the degree to which they can Enclose and Direct their Attention, pull back a little in order to face each other and smile, and then finally kiss. To be hugged by someone who performs it as a Gesture, however, is noticeably different. The arms will enclose and the head incline without the rest of the body following. To the onlooker it may look a sincere, warm hug, but to the recipient it will feel cold and meaningless. Most of all there will be no Flow, none of the Growing/Shrinking or Freeing/Binding as the embrace progresses as there is between lovers. There are, of course, tremendous cultural differences between acceptable levels of contact on introduction, varying between a formal bow with no physical contact to three kisses on the cheeks now expected in Switzerland. Not to know the rules can lead to embarrassment and even ridicule.

We can see therefore that affinities are expected to occur in a person's behaviour between Effort and Shape, and that Posture is expected to merge with Gesture or Gesture with Posture. An Effort movement which is not appropriately matched by a Shape movement will result in some form of clumsiness, whereas a Shape movement without its affinity in Effort will appear listless. A person with fully integrated behaviour in terms of strong affinities between Shape and Effort or with clear merging of Posture and Gesture will project a very clear image of themselves. They are likely to be popular because people feel they know what they are dealing with, where they stand.

The adult movement pattern is not entirely rigid, but only slight variations will take place during a person's lifetime without the intervention of some trauma. The relationship of one plane of movement to the others, once established in adult life, will remain fairly constant. Any attempt to develop a particular range of movement, perhaps for therapeutic reasons, should not threaten this basic relationship according to Warren Lamb. To introduce or force upon someone movement which unbalances their established movement pattern causes stress and possibly personality disturbance. A person forced to behave by pressure from say a parent or employer, in a way unnatural to them is being forced to be someone they are not. The discomfort and stress may be mental, but has its roots equally in the physical stress of trying, say, to make demure and submissive movements when there is an assertive personality clamouring for attention, or to behave in a quick and decisive manner when they are by nature laid back and exploratory.

In summary then, making an aptitude assessment of an individual had by 1960 developed into observation of six categories of behaviour:

| Posture and Shape | Gesture and Shape | Flow of Shape |
| Posture and Effort | Gesture and Effort | Flow of Effort |

The observations taken in each category would then be analysed in order to find the Posture Gesture Mergers, and to produce a diagram to show visually the degree of movement in each of the six ranges of Shape and Effort. [Fig. 8]

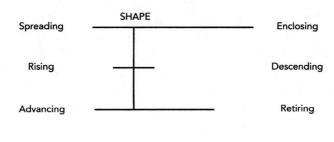

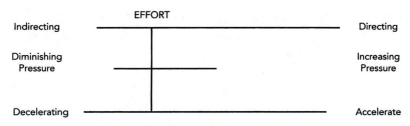

Fig. 8. An imaginary individual's movement graph

Set out numerically the same information would look something like this:

Movements recorded		Frequency/Total no/%
SHAPE		
Horizontal plane	Spreading	27 } = 37 [15%]
	Enclosing	10 }
Vertical plane	Rising	4 } = 8 [3%]
	Descending	4 }
Saggital	Advancing	13 } = 38 [15%]
	Retiring	25 }
EFFORT		
Space	Indirecting	15 }
	Directing	47 } = 62 [25%]
Weight	Diminishing pressure	10 }
	Increasing pressure	20 } = 30 [12%]
Time	Decelerating	20 }
	Accelerating	55 } = 75 [30%]
Total number of observations taken		250 [100%]

From the information collected here we can work out a thumb-nail sketch of an individual who is so strong in the Commitment stage he or she is more eager to leap into action than to work out the whys and wherefores. Whilst he/she is rich in Directing activity, seeking information, this is not sufficiently combined with the necessary affinity in Shape of Enclosing which would ensure that the knowledge gained was given any sort of structure and the low activity in the Intention band accentuates this easy-going lack of discrimination. The strong affinity in the Sagittal range, however, does indicate a great strength in anything requiring timing, decision-taking and possibly creativity.

This, then, is the type of information Warren Lamb gleaned from a 1- to 2-hour interview. When it was presented to the client it would take a detailed form such as that shown in Appendix III.

INTO TEAM-BUILDING

The importance of the affinities between Shape and Effort in a person's behaviour and the discovery of the PGM factor in movement, led to another substantial step forward. This was the tremendous amount that could now be deduced about a person's potential, not simply in a particular job situation, but in their ability to operate as part of a senior management team.

Team building had already been practiced at the operative level, notably for Faithful Ltd in the early 1950s. Advice had also been given with every assessment for industry on how managers would be likely to act and interact with their colleagues, particularly where it would be necessary for workmates to be ready to compensate for their "Weaknesses".

The analysis of affinities between a person's Shape and Effort it was now realised, put together with the degree of Flow, gives sensitive information on that person's ability to interact with others. If a person was high in Investigating Effort, but low in either Spreading or Enclosing Shape, this might mean that the results of their "Investigation", their research, would never be communicated to his/her colleagues, that this person had a low potential for Sharing. Warren Lamb began an analysis of the qualities needed in team-building among senior executives, and this then became one of the most enduring cornerstones of his work.

To use this system for selecting and placing people in senior positions was no "quick fix". It involved possibly a two hour initial interview with each of the candidates and colleagues of the appointee. The procedure would end with follow-up interviews with the successful candidate and those with whom he would be working to advise them on what to expect of each other, together with all the relevant lengthy reports. It was nevertheless found to be highly effective and accurate, and once a company began to use him, Warren Lamb was usually retained for many years.

In the early days of working on his own as a Management Consultant, Warren Lamb liked to have someone else in the room to engage the candidate in conversation while he made his observations. Later he was to perfect a technique of both interviewing and making notations simultaneously, even though it meant that he might momentarily lose the drift of what had just been said as he concentrated on notating the movement.

The Managing Director of Trebor, Colonel Sydney Marks, was one of the early people to use his services for team-building. Having learnt what Movement Analysis was about Marks invited Lamb to make an assessment of him and his Production Manager, Peter Kenyon. It was fortunate that on this occasion there were two subjects who could talk to each other while Warren Lamb made notes.

This exercise was particularly significant in that it was probably the first application of Movement Pattern Analysis to team-building at a senior level. The movement patterns of both men were observed while they talked to each other. It seemed to Lamb that the same principles applied at the executive as at the shop-floor level. Some people move relatively in harmony with each other and some in disharmony. Elements of both exist in all relationships, and disharmony [what Laban liked to call lopsidedness or disequilibrium] is not always a negative quality. The essential thing was to explain to the client in which activities there was likely to be good teamwork and in which not.

Marks and Kenyon accepted the observations Lamb presented to them with his demonstrations, and were able then to discuss ways of dealing with the shortcomings in their working relationship and to build on their strengths. For example Lamb suggested that one problem was that Marks made 'mountains out of molehills', so that Kenyon never knew which was the most important thing to be getting on with. They therefore discussed ways in which Marks could prioritise so that Kenyon knew if he was dealing with a mountain or a molehill. Working relations between the two men improved considerably although they still had their ups and downs. The improvement was significant enough for Lamb to be asked to look at team-building within Trebor and also to give guidance throughout their senior levels, with a view to making for better teamwork and releasing individual potential. Sydney Marks would park his Rolls Royce outside Warren Lamb's rooms in Portland Place, and climb the 84 stairs for a movement session, as did many Trebor executives for several years.

In the team-building work Warren Lamb does now there might be less actual movement training, but the results are remarkably successful. When one considers the lengths some companies go to in order to promote team spirit, with strenuous, sometimes dangerous Outward Bound activities, Movement Analysis looks so much simpler.

Team-building based on Movement Pattern Analysis deals with the basic influence of harmony – the feed-back to one's Kinaesthetic Sense from working in close proximity with other people. It affects our behaviour even when the other person is not there but has to be taken into account, and it affects the ease or otherwise of communication. Remarkably there is sometimes more effective communication between people who appear to be in conflict with each other than between people who claim to like each other. Teamwork is a dynamic, ranging this way and that and static definition of roles is of limited use in such a fluid situation.

Following the work started at Trebor, Warren Lamb increasingly had a reputation as the person to advise on short-listed candidates for management and executive positions, and in all cases he gave great importance to the nature of the team the candidate would have to work with. Concepts of Team-Fit and Team-Mix began to emerge.

By now Movement Pattern Analysis had moved on a considerable distance from the simple tool used by Laban to relieve stress and improve efficiency in the Mars operation. If it was doubtful then that someone without movement training could identify what was required, it is even more improbable that a person without considerable training could identify Posture and Gesture, Effort and Shape, and then determine how much Flow a movement contained, let alone interpret their findings.

By 1965 when Warren Lamb published *Posture and Gesture* he had arrived at his own technique of notation and analysis. Laban's method of notation including the basic Effort symbols had been adapted, and Lamb had developed an ability to interview and notate at the same time. Although he had taken Labanotation and Movement Analysis so much further, he is the first to acknowledge the huge debt he owes to the original work done by Laban in not only devising the original Labanotation, but also in seeing the huge potential of movement study.

Critical to the value of both was the sound philosophical basis from which Laban worked. Lamb had not left his origins behind. He was still involved with alumni of the Movement Studio, and with various summer schools in movement and dance which continued to thrive. But his feet were firmly on a path to use movement study to understand human potential, and to use this as a management tool.

Later he had this to say about Laban: "I look upon him as one of the few truly creative geniuses who ever existed, because most work that is done which is often regarded as original has stemmed from something else. But Laban was truly creative, truly original, and I think we are still reeling from the scope and quality of what it is that he opened up ... He left it to other people to work it through, to clarify or systematise his ideas. Laban himself never wanted to systematise his ideas." [Interviews of Warren Lamb by Susan M. Lovell, *American Journal of Dance Therapy*. Spring/Summer 1993 Vol.15 No.1]

CHAPTER FIVE

ACTION PROFILERS INTERNATIONAL

BROADENING THE BASE: PAMELA RAMSDEN

By the 1960s Warren Lamb worked largely in management selection, and increasingly with only senior executives. As Warren Lamb Associates he had various partners each contributing their own skills, but Aptitude Assessment was always the leading edge of the management consultancy and its main selling point. Aptitude Assessment was used as a selection technique, and for advising companies on executive team-building. An off-shoot for a while was also an individual career guidance service.

At a financial low-point in 1965 Executive Search – head-hunting – was added to the products offered and became a lucrative part of the Warren Lamb Associates' operation. The same method of assessment by movement observation was used for this. His reputation was such by now that he was sometimes asked to select from a short list of candidates put up by other recruitment agencies, and on occasion advised against appointing anyone on their list. At the same time seminars and conferences on Movement Analysis and Aptitude Assessment continued to spread the word and to drum up business.

The roots in Laban were always maintained. Many of Laban's pupils, now working in other fields, came to him for training in the early 60s, feeling, quite justifiably, that Warren had had special access to Laban during his latter years. Among them were Laban's daughter Juana de Laban, Irmgard Bartenieff, Dr Judith Kestenberg, and Betty Meredith Jones to mention a few. It was working with them, he later said, which forced him to clarify for himself what he was doing, and a direct outcome of that was his identification of the Posture Gesture Merger, the essential core of his movement analysis. Posture Gesture Mergers were not inventions he said, but the formulation of what had always been observed. "It was there all the time. It is rooted in Laban's teachings. But it had not been succinctly expressed." Significant was the realisation that here was a part of movement behaviour which no one can fake, and which therefore gives the most reliable information about the interviewee.

No sooner had Warren Lamb Associates added Executive Search to their bow, with a great deal of lucrative success, than there was a tremendous flurry of activity. *Posture and Gesture*, published in 1965, created a lot of interest and Warren Lamb had television programmes such as *Tomorrow's World* and *Horizon* devoted solely to him, as well as numerous other television and radio interviews. Within the year his financial situation had turned round.

The lack of independent validation was still a worry, however, as was the fact that Warren Lamb was still the only practitioner of his techniques. In recent years the need to earn to pay school fees for four children and the mortgage had been too pressing to take time off to devise lengthy training and validation exercises. Both these problems had to be addressed in the next decade.

In 1970 Warren Lamb Associates was joined by Pamela Ramsden, a psychology graduate of Melbourne University, who had spent a year studying Movement Analysis at the Art of Movement Studio, Addlestone. Initially she was employed by Trebor [now part of Cadbury and a long-standing client of Warren Lamb Associates] who were eager to sponsor validation research into Aptitude Assessment. She first tried to do this by means of questionnaires and taped interviews with colleagues of people who had previously been assessed to gain feedback on their behaviour. The questionnaires brought little quantifiable response; not surprisingly she found that any information gained told her more about the manager being questioned than about the person they were supposed to be reporting on. Such was her enthusiasm however, that she persuaded Warren to train her in observing movement, and immediately with two people competent at observation and notation, it was possible to make some sort of beginning at one important aspect of validation – inter-observer reliability.

Whilst the consultancy work went on apace, the early 70s saw a lot of experimenting with various structures for courses and interviews, with methods of report writing, and with training schemes for new observers. Managers were trained to check the reliability of their own assessments. Other experiments tested the length of time it was necessary to observe a person in order to see a full range of their behaviour before the true ratio of the elements of their movement emerged. The time proved to be one and a half to two hours, exactly the time Warren himself had always used. Research was also undertaken to validate his premise that a person's movement pattern once formed did not change over a period of time. Candidates were chosen whom Warren Lamb had assessed years earlier, and they were now re-assessed several times over the period of a year and under different conditions. The findings again bore out Warren Lamb's contention that the movement pattern, the ratio between the various elements of Effort, Shape and Flow, once established in childhood is with us more or less for life.

In 1971 Pamela Ramsden became a partner in Warren Lamb Associates. Two years later she published *Top Team Planning*, demonstrating the direction which Aptitude Assessment, now given the name Action Profiling, was taking. Action Profiling was a diagnostic tool still entirely based on notation of Effort, Shape and Flow, on Posture/Gesture Merging, and the Decision-Making Process. It differed only in its greater emphasis on executive team building — by now the most expanding area of their work.

All the elements of Action Profiling had been identified over the previous twenty years. In *Action News* [Winter 1981] Warren Lamb described them as being in place as early as 1965, although they may not have been so clearly formulated:

1. The concept of a decision-making sequence enabling emphasis to be put on the process as distinct from the content of a decision.
2. The isolation of posture-gesture-merging ... containing the relatively enduring features of a person's individual movement ...
3. The systematic matching of Effort [assertion] with Shape [perspective].
4. The notion of affinities between Effort and Shape having significance for interaction.
5. The distinction between two types of Flow, Flow of Effort and Flow of Shape, essential for the concept of 'Identifying'...
6. The Framework which divides the three-stage decision-making process into six basic actions and the three interactions together with three overall factors [Dynamism, Adaptability and Identifying].
7. The recognition that Flow [of Effort and Shape] diminishes during childhood growth while Effort and Shaping movement of the three stages of the decision-making process are being developed.

The methods of interview and movement notation used in Action Profiling were exactly the same as those developed by Warren Lamb for Aptitude Assessment. Only the form of report writing was changed to include more data relating to executive interaction. What the system lacked, however, was a basis in academic recognition. Without doubt it worked, but still too few people knew how, and even less knew why.

The contribution required of Pamela Ramsden and in part delivered, was to promote movement analysis by giving it a broader basis of validation and by substantially increasing the number of practitioners. The focus, however, was still entirely on Executive Selection, the most lucrative way in which assessments could be used. Terminology was changed, ideas were regrouped for evermore sophisticated interpretations, with the inevitable danger that the original principles would be obscured.

THE BODY/MIND CONNECTION

The Body/Mind aspect of Movement Analysis and its psychological features were elucidated by Pamela Ramsden as a result of her own training and, possibly also of visits she and Warren Lamb made to Judith Kestenberg and Irmgaard Bartenieff, movement therapists working in New York. One typical development was that Ramsden came to the conclusion that what was being measured was not Aptitude but Motivation, and Motivation to Act [Fig. 9] became the report description of managerial behaviour. The Body/Mind area had been largely neglected by Laban's pupils in his dance studios. The intuitive understanding between expressive movement and thought is the basis of dance. When a dancer represents anger or tranquillity we are in no doubt what thought process he is representing. Similarly our own actions are determined by the complication of emotions directing our "performance".

Through Pamela Ramsden attention was given to the nature of the relationship between movement and thought. It was her belief that when a particular quality of movement integrates posture and gesture, the experience "triggers" a related conscious thought process and vice versa. Warren Lamb never described it as so sequential. Although he fully accepts the relationship of thought/action, he has always seen the process as a more complicated amalgam of simultaneous events.

Given this difference, both Ramsden and Lamb accept as natural a body/mind relationship, that a Directing Effort, for example, should be related to and enable focussed thinking. If a movement is integrated in a Directing way, it is probably impossible at the same time for the person to be thinking in a wandering, unfocussed fashion. Such a contradiction could only happen if the person deliberately isolated parts of the body, and to do that would not allow any coherent thought or action to take place.

This again was not a discovery, but the identification of something which had been known by Laban at the outset, and which it was now helpful to the purpose of Action Profiling to elucidate. The notion identifies the basis of Laban's teaching. If a person is by nature Exploratory, but by his or her work is required to be highly focussed, for example on small parts of machinery or on sets of closely argued figures, that person will be stressed by their work and will over a period of time inevitably perform poorly.

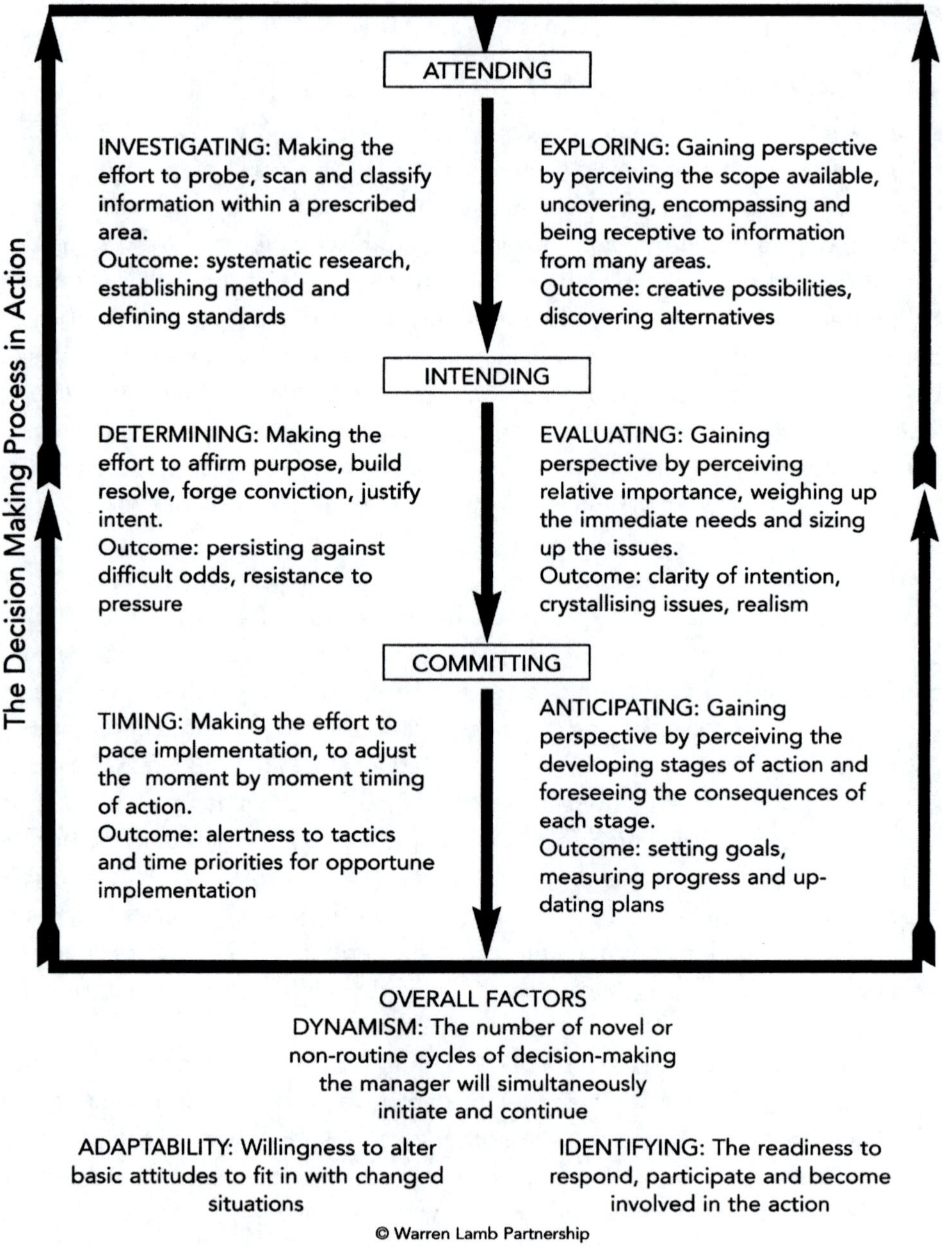

The Decision Making Process in Action

ATTENDING

INVESTIGATING: Making the effort to probe, scan and classify information within a prescribed area.
Outcome: systematic research, establishing method and defining standards

EXPLORING: Gaining perspective by perceiving the scope available, uncovering, encompassing and being receptive to information from many areas.
Outcome: creative possibilities, discovering alternatives

INTENDING

DETERMINING: Making the effort to affirm purpose, build resolve, forge conviction, justify intent.
Outcome: persisting against difficult odds, resistance to pressure

EVALUATING: Gaining perspective by perceiving relative importance, weighing up the immediate needs and sizing up the issues.
Outcome: clarity of intention, crystallising issues, realism

COMMITTING

TIMING: Making the effort to pace implementation, to adjust the moment by moment timing of action.
Outcome: alertness to tactics and time priorities for opportune implementation

ANTICIPATING: Gaining perspective by perceiving the developing stages of action and foreseeing the consequences of each stage.
Outcome: setting goals, measuring progress and up-dating plans

OVERALL FACTORS
DYNAMISM: The number of novel or non-routine cycles of decision-making the manager will simultaneously initiate and continue

ADAPTABILITY: Willingness to alter basic attitudes to fit in with changed situations

IDENTIFYING: The readiness to respond, participate and become involved in the action

© Warren Lamb Partnership

Fig. 9. Framework of Management Initiative: The Motivation to Act

THE MOTIVATION TO INTERACT

Emphasis upon the executive as part of a team, already a substantial part of the work of Warren Lamb, became the major selling point of Action Profiling. The Framework of Management Initiative he had devised was now sub-titled Motivation to Act [Fig.9], and joined by a second Framework, the Motivation to Interact [Fig.10]. The nature of a person's Action Profile it was claimed, would also show his/her potential for interaction with colleagues.

Using the 12 polarities of Shape and Effort and the 4 polarities of Flow, it was postulated that an effective team should have a good balance of all qualities in its members, and that for a team to be effective there should be at least 10% of each polarity in its make-up. The validity of this was shown by three experiments reported by Tim Lamb [Warren's son] in his Master's thesis for Imperial College, London. The results of the experiments are amusing and seem to bear out the Action Profiling theory that effective teams must have a good range of types for effective decisions to result from their efforts.

The experiments were set up with groups of people from some of Warren Lamb's client companies. In the first experiment twelve executives from CIGA hotels were divided into three groups of four people according to their Action Profiles. In other words, one group was of people all strong in the Attention range, a second in the Intention range, and the third in the Commitment range. No account was taken of their positions in the company.

Experiment One
Each group was asked to "appoint a group leader to report back initiatives which your company can take for improved strategy on security".
Attention Group
The report from this group listed 27 different definitions of kinds of security and the company's responsibility. Through a spokesman they recommended a research group should be set up to look into the matter and report back in 3 months.
Intention group
Through its spokesman this group recommended that a security manager should be appointed at each of the company's hotels, with extensive definitions of what his function and authority should be. Points on which the group had disagreed were listed.
Commitment group
This group recommended that a recently introduced staff training scheme should be expanded to educate all staff on security matters, and that the current building

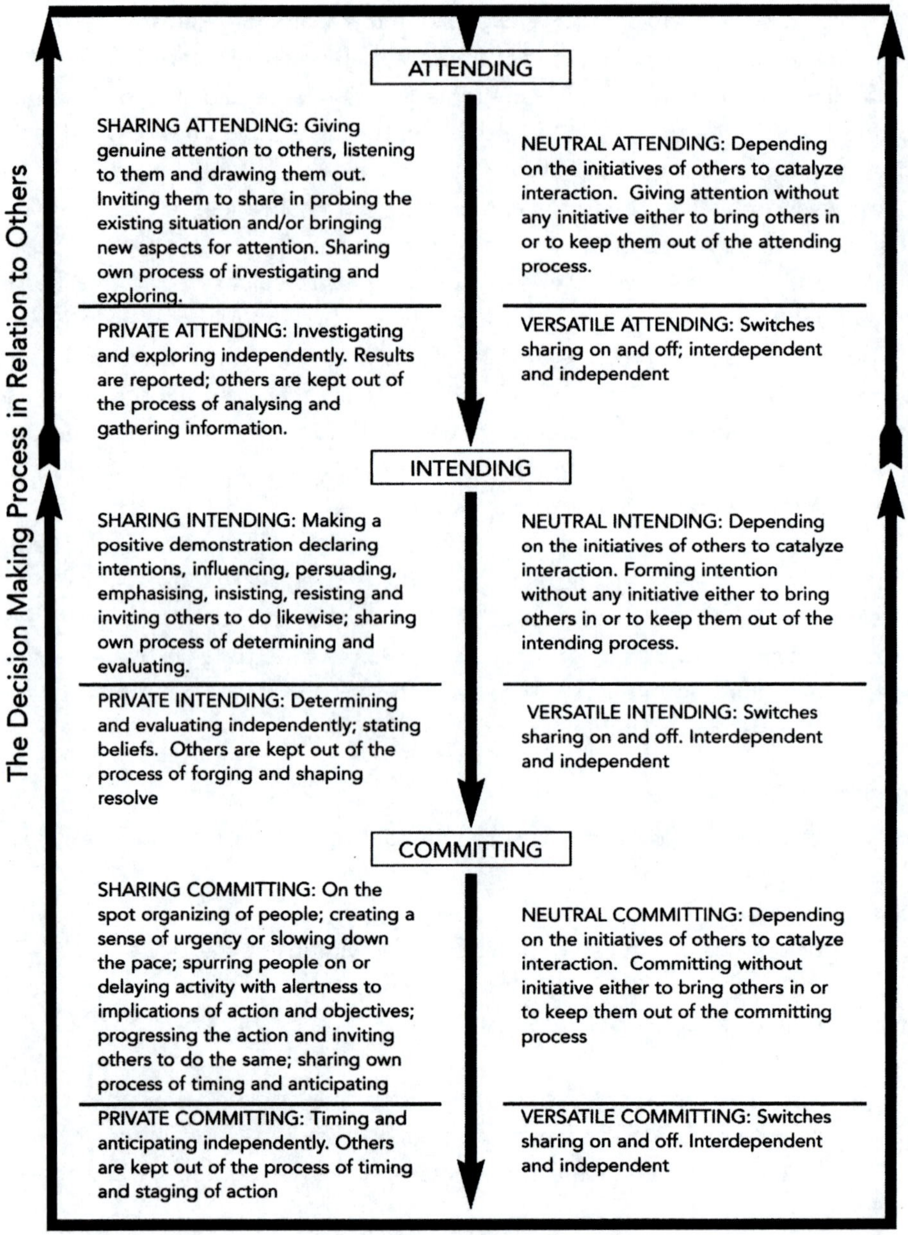

The Decision Making Process in Relation to Others

ATTENDING

SHARING ATTENDING: Giving genuine attention to others, listening to them and drawing them out. Inviting them to share in probing the existing situation and/or bringing new aspects for attention. Sharing own process of investigating and exploring.

NEUTRAL ATTENDING: Depending on the initiatives of others to catalyze interaction. Giving attention without any initiative either to bring others in or to keep them out of the attending process.

PRIVATE ATTENDING: Investigating and exploring independently. Results are reported; others are kept out of the process of analysing and gathering information.

VERSATILE ATTENDING: Switches sharing on and off; interdependent and independent

INTENDING

SHARING INTENDING: Making a positive demonstration declaring intentions, influencing, persuading, emphasising, insisting, resisting and inviting others to do likewise; sharing own process of determining and evaluating.

NEUTRAL INTENDING: Depending on the initiatives of others to catalyze interaction. Forming intention without any initiative either to bring others in or to keep them out of the intending process.

PRIVATE INTENDING: Determining and evaluating independently; stating beliefs. Others are kept out of the process of forging and shaping resolve

VERSATILE INTENDING: Switches sharing on and off. Interdependent and independent

COMMITTING

SHARING COMMITTING: On the spot organizing of people; creating a sense of urgency or slowing down the pace; spurring people on or delaying activity with alertness to implications of action and objectives; progressing the action and inviting others to do the same; sharing own process of timing and anticipating

NEUTRAL COMMITTING: Depending on the initiatives of others to catalyze interaction. Committing without initiative either to bring others in or to keep them out of the committing process

PRIVATE COMMITTING: Timing and anticipating independently. Others are kept out of the process of timing and staging of action

VERSATILE COMMITTING: Switches sharing on and off. Interdependent and independent

© Warren Lamb Partnership

Fig. 10. Framework of Management Initiative: The Motivation to Interact

and conversion programme should introduce improved security measures wherever possible. It was suggested these changes should have immediate effect, but no details of the changes were presented.

Experiment Two

In this experiment twelve executives from Albany International New York headquarters divided into similar groups were asked to "appoint a group leader to report on initiatives for improving inter-company transfers of personnel".

Attention Group

This group reported an unfinished discussion on the principles involved in moving people around the world, often into strange cultures, and with strain upon the family. The group reached no conclusion, and no recommendations were made.

Intention Group

This group declared emphatically what should and should not be done, mostly the latter, and gave examples of transfers they believed would be wrong.

Commitment Group

In this group the managers made thirty-three quick-fire recommendations for steps to make inter-company transfers more acceptable.

Experiment Three

Similar results were forthcoming from the third experiment conducted with a division of Albany International, where the groups had to discuss the desirability of designating the Christmas leave as a paid holiday. In this case the Attention group questioned what the employees would do with the holiday and feared they might simply get drunk, whilst the Intention group urged the company to withstand pressure from the staff to make the change. The Commitment group, however, thought the company should change the rules of the holiday immediately as this was the growing trend in the business.

THE OVERALL FACTORS

Another feature of Action Profiling with its emphasis on teamwork was the use of the Overall Factors: Adaptability, Dynamism and Identification. Again these were not new concepts but they became important elements in the Motivation to Act as qualities believed to have an over-riding effect on how a manager uses his other capacities. [Fig.9]

In *Management Behaviour* in 1969, co-written by Warren Lamb and David Turner, then a partner in Warren Lamb Associates, Adaptability, Dynamism and

Identification had already been defined. For Action Profiling Dynamism was rated on a scale of one to ten and Adaptability and Identification as High or Low. The measurement of the qualities was intended to be a descriptive rather than a qualitative judgement and had to be seen in relation to all other aspects of a person's profile. In *Top Team Planning* Pamela Ramsden gave them lengthier and more specific definitions. As further aspects of behaviour analysis they can be interesting in broader terms than simply for executive performance.

Adaptability

Adaptability is seen as the motivation to change basic attitudes to meet differing situations. In a company doing anything other than standing still, be it thriving or failing, there will be constant change. A quality worth measuring is, therefore, the ability of a person to handle change – their Adaptability. A highly adaptable manager should be able to change his role and attitudes to meet a new situation, rather than take umbrage or perhaps try to change the situation to suit himself. In movement terms a close affinity between Effort and Shape indicates Adaptability. With this a person finds it easy to progress from one stage of the Decision-Making Process to the next. Where there is low or no affinity behaviour is liable to be disjointed and disorganised in unusual situations. That is not the whole picture, of course, as Ramsden points out. It is still necessary to know in which parts of the Decision-Making Process the person is strong or weak in order to know what they will do with their ability to adapt. It is also necessary to know what the circumstances are in which they will have to operate and how relevant their Adaptability will be in the situation. A person high in Adaptability may institute change just for the sake of it – a temptation for all executives in a new post. At a later date Carol Lynne Moore was to argue that this Overall Factor should be abandoned as, unlike the others, it is deduced from looking at the whole Action Profile already made and not directly from movement observation itself.

Dynamism

Dynamism is the degree to which the individual can operate several aspects of the Decision-Making Process simultaneously. In talking about movement Warren Lamb constantly stresses that movement is movement and not fixed positions; how we arrive in a position and go from it to the next is the only significance. It follows that in order for movement to continue, every movement must at some point be reversed even if it is only in order to do it again. If a person puts on increasing pressure, perhaps to emphasise an argument, they must eventually decrease that pressure or else arrive in a state of paralysis. A person who has more than the norm of reversals of Effort or Shape in this sense is a person with more than the norm in Dynamism. They will give the impression of being a go-getter, of having terrific energy. It is a highly desirable quality in a manager in most cases. These are the people who by literally over-coming inertia, can turn around stagnant situations and can handle several non-routine decision-making situations at once. To Laban it was energetically "loaded" movement, and something which, according to Warren Lamb's analysis of Laban [Appendix 1], he possessed. His high Dynamism, Sharing and Commitment all combined to give him the charisma so many found irresistible.

A person high in Dynamism can be assertive in many different ways simultaneously. They can, for example, take the initiative with penetrating insight and with authority. In doing so they can sweep colleagues along with their drive, but dangerously, they can easily usurp their power and overstep the mark. Pamela Ramsden points out the potential downside with this sort of person. It is essential that the dynamic manager has [or has access to through colleagues] all the other attributes to suit the situation. "A dynamic but unintelligent manager may be deadly – a bit like a high powered car with an idiot for a driver".

Identification

Simply put, Identification is the extent to which the person is motivated to take part in the Decision-Making Process. It indicates his or her willingness to wholly participate in the activity of an organisation, to take on board its aims and traditions, to fit into the environment and be an involved member of a team. Our perception of a person's ability to 'join in' in this way is determined by the degree of Flow in their movement, whether this is Flow of Shape [Growing or Shrinking] or Flow of Effort [Freeing or Binding]. As explained earlier, Flow is the quality of movement infants are born with which is gradually replaced by the development of Effort and Shape as we approach adulthood. It is largely determined therefore by childhood experience. Retaining a fair amount of Flow gives movement a more spontaneous and participatory appearance. A lack of Flow on the other hand gives an impression of aloofness. Either quality may be useful in different situations, but on the whole the observer would be happier to see a greater variation in Flow in a candidate joining a team.

Warren Lamb sees the degree of Identification in a company as something which affects its whole culture. He quotes cases of companies low in Identification where each person is concerned only with their immediate area, and primarily with their own career. A case in point was IBM in the 1980s, a company noted for its cut and thrust. To move from such a company to one with High Identification was a hard, almost impossible, adjustment to make. Hewlett Packard was an example of a company where each person had a strong sense of being part of the whole structure, especially encouraged by their policy of senior managers "walking around" at given times of the day and seeing everyone in their department.

Families, like companies, also operate with varying degrees of Identification. Some have very 'tribal' behaviour handed down through generations. The motto is almost "All for one and one for all". The same can apply to schools, clubs and the armed services, and it is not everyone who feels comfortable belonging to this kind of organisation whilst for others it is the only way to exist. At the same time it is fairly commonly accepted that many social problems are the result of a breakdown in the traditional infrastructure of family/community/religion. The two-way process of upholding group values on the one hand, or being answerable to caring peers and relatives for one's behaviour on the other, often no longer operates.

SHARING AND PRIVATE BEHAVIOUR

Notions of Sharing and Private behaviour had also been described by Warren Lamb and David Turner in the 1960s. These were now incorporated into the Motivation to Interact by Pamela Ramsden [together with another Profiler and member of Warren Lamb Associates, Eddie Bows] and given the new title of Preferred Interactional Style.

The theory of Sharing and Private behaviour concerns the degree to which a person prefers to work independently or as part of a team and is therefore crucial to their Motivation to Interact [Fig.10]. This varies not only between individuals but also in one person at each stage of the Decision-Making Process. It is obviously extremely valuable for employers to know at what point a manager is liable to be either secretive or cooperative. One person may be happy to share in the Attention Stage, inviting others to cooperate in finding out the whole picture or investigating a situation, and will together with others decide the rights and wrongs [Intention Stage], but will suddenly astound their colleagues when [in the Commitment Stage] they go off and single-handedly take action.

Strong affinities in any one range of Shape and Effort encourage an attitude of Sharing, of inviting co-operation in that stage. In the Attention Stage affinity in a person gives the message that they are comfortably at ease and easily accessible. A lack of affinity would suggest aloofness or a desire for Privacy, which may simply mean that the individual was holding back until he felt more familiar with the situation.

To Sharing and Private Ramsden and Bowes added two further concepts of Neutral and Versatile. "Neutral" behaviour would be that of a person who showed no capacity to either Share or be Private, one who simply went along with the mode of operation and did not try to change anything. The "Versatile" person on the other hand will literally switch on and off between Sharing and Private behaviour. According to how the manager uses his/her Versatility, colleagues could feel confused as to how he/she would behave on any given day or issue. If it was used responsibly however, it could be a sensitive way of responding to other people's needs.

Some of the differences at each stage of the Decision-Making Process where each type of behaviour is present can be summarised, as follows.

Attention Stage

Sharing: a willingness to contribute ideas and information and a receptiveness to others' suggestions, making colleagues feel valued.
Private: independence in pursuing research and using only formal methods for giving and receiving information.

Intention Stage

Sharing: the person will involve colleagues in his/her pursuit of information and try to influence them as to priorities. Will be open but persuasive.
Private: this person will be aloof and a 'loner', unwilling to go beyond formal statements and reluctant to change his/her stance. Will inspire either deference or resentment.

Commitment Stage

Sharing: very concerned with timing and objectives, and will try to instill the same concern in colleagues. May be more concerned with the speed of the task than how it is done. Can create a lively working environment but can also put subordinates under stress.
Private: colleagues may feel he/she might inadvertently go behind their backs in pursuit of his/her own goals. Tim Lamb cites the example of General de Gaulle who left his ministers in the dark on several important issues of

French foreign policy. In 1966 they learned of France's imminent withdrawal from NATO three days after the American President had been informed.

By the time all these aspects of a person's character had been examined and put together with data on experience and qualifications there was little left to know about a candidate. Information collected in an interview was tabulated into various diagrams and charts [see Fig. 11] which on the face of it left little to the imagination. The validity of any of it of course depended entirely on the accuracy of the original observations made in interview, and the interpretation of those findings. It was tempting to codify and give numerical quantities to as many aspects of behaviour as possible, but the apparent clarity gained by doing so was in itself possibly the antitheses of what human behaviour is really like. Warren Lamb never lost sight of this fact.

TRAINING PROFILERS

After the publication of *Top Team Planning* Pamela Ramsden continued to train as an observer by working alongside Warren Lamb. At the same time she set up several experiments in various types of training. There was, most of all she felt, a need to find a method of training which was quicker than the sit-alongside system she had had to use and to this end she successfully set about creating a range of training materials. Intensive 5 day courses were set up for teams of managers to help them understand their own Profiles. Videos were made of them performing tasks requiring Attention, Intention and Commitment, and these were then studied and analysed. Warren Lamb had always been extremely cautious about the value of film as an observation aid as it tended to distort or flatten Effort. In experiments in training Ramsden found it suitable only when the 'live' movement had already been observed.

At first she thought it unnecessary to teach movement in order to train people in observation, but eventually she found that some training in the scales of movement was essential. A favoured way of teaching an appreciation of movement was found to be to start with large exaggerated movements and gradually arrive at 'normal' sized replicas of the same movement, a method used frequently by Warren Lamb.

Slowly the number of Profilers built up. Not everyone who came for training proved to have the necessary Kinaesthetic Sense to make good observers, but there were some notable successes such as Carol Lynne Moore, Eddie Bows and Ellen Goodman who were soon helping with courses. By 1980 a more formal pattern of training and organisation was emerging. A course consisting of three two-day sessions was pioneered. Its syllabus included making and interpreting profiles,

JOHN SMITH		% of total activity		Extent of interaction activity	
Assertion	Perspective			Sharing	Private
Investigating		27	Communicating	80	
ATTENTION					50
	Exploring	23			
Determining		14	Presenting	70	70
INTENTION					
	Evaluating	20			
Timing		6	Operating		80
COMMITMENT					
	Anticipating	10		20	
Assertion/Perspective ratio		47/53			
Dynamism on a ten-point scale		6			
Adaptability		High			
Identifying		Medium			

Fig. 11. Tabular presentation of an Action Profile

counselling, report-writing and conducting team-building assignments. On a trip to New York, Pamela Ramsden and Warren Lamb visited the Effort and Shape Department of the Dance Notation Bureau. This later became the Laban Institute of Movement Studies and after that the Laban/Bartenieff Institute. The outcome of the visit was a successful series of training courses in New York and the formation of the North American branch of Action Profiling. A branch was also formed in South Africa.

An informal organisation calling itself Action Profilers International was set up in 1978, becoming official in 1981 with Warren Lamb as its President. By 1983 it had 30 members working in the United Kingdom, the United States, Europe and South Africa. In June, Action News, which had till then been published by Warren Lamb Associates, was taken over by API, edited by Carol Lynne Moore. The mission statement in that edition read:

"Action Profilers International is a professional membership organisation established to further the development of techniques of behavioural analysis known as Action Profiling. Primary organisational objectives of API include setting standards of competence for Action Profile Practitioners, promoting the use and development of Action Profiling for the benefit of commerce and industry, advancing research on the Profile and disseminating information to the public."

Action Profiling International grew and consolidated during the 1980s with ever increasing interest and activity. Annual conferences were held as far afield as Colorado, Holland, Belgium, Swaziland, New York and London. A training system was developed for two levels of Profiler, Member and Associate, where trainees to qualify as a fully certified Action Profiler [a Member] had to achieve at least .85 correlation with their trainer on at least three consecutive subjects, after making at least 20 Profiles under close supervision. Controls were operated by a Training Committee and a Standards Committee. The General Council to which one could only aspire after at least two years as a Member, met twice a year, once in the spring and once before the autumn Annual Conference.

RESEARCH AND VALIDATION

More scientific validation was still necessary and to this end a research project was carried out by Deborah du Nann Winter and others of Whitman College, Washington into Posture/Gesture Mergers. It was published in the Winter 1989 *Journal of Non Verbal Behaviour*.

Four experiments were carried out for which judges received fifteen hours training over a five week period. They watched a number of practice videos of people being interviewed, where only the person being interviewed was on the screen, and no sound was used. A series of exercises helped them to identify PGMs, and reliability tests checked the success of the training before they proceeded to the experiments.

In the first experiment interviewees were instructed to lie about their opinions on the subject for discussion for a certain length of time, and then to tell the truth. The results supported Lamb's theory that PGMs are the result of sincere not contrived behaviour, and therefore that observation of them can be used as a 'lie detector'. The second experiment aimed to find out if PGMs occurred more in relaxed than in tense behaviour. One group was treated to 45 minutes lying on the floor listening to music and instruction on how to relax various muscles, while the other sat at desks studying for 45 minutes. The group members were then interviewed. Generally the premise was supported by the findings, but at first the "relaxing" group were too sleepy to do anything much at all! The interviewees were next subjected to various degrees of frustration with a task involving putting balls into slots on a tray under different degrees of pressure, and in the fourth experiment an outside "Rater" knowing nothing about PGMs was asked to identify points of sincerity and authenticity in a videotaped debating tournament, and this was then matched against the occurrence of PGMs. The results of these two experiments again positively supported Warren Lamb's beliefs that frustration reduces the occurrence of PGMs and that behaviour containing PGMs is perceived as sincere and authentic. Deborah du Nann Winter added the caution that there was ample room for further research to examine other aspects of the system's validity.

She was equally cautious with her conclusions on her research into Action Profiling itself. Whilst generally the results proved the validity of the link between cognitive behaviour and body movement, she stressed that the system is carefully honed for commercial use and therefore there was no research to validate it for more general application.

Research, reported in *The Body-Mind Connection in Human Movement Analysis* [ed. Susan Loman 1992], again describes experiments designed to test the reliability of Action Profiling. The first experiment tested inter-judge reliability and found this to be good. This was despite a tendency for the Profilers to recognise movement from their own profiles more easily than movement which they did not themselves have. The second experiment tested the link between movement and thinking processes and found the match "highly significant". A third experiment found a favourable comparison between the results from Action Profiling and results when the same subjects were given the Myers Briggs Inventory, a system of measuring similar aspects of personal aptitudes, also based on Jungian psychology.

A further experiment tested the notion that people with certain abilities will be found in careers requiring those aptitudes. This would test Lamb's contention that once formed the individual's PGM endures and "is a deep motivational force in a person's life to particular behaviour ... [and we have] an inbuilt compulsion to arrange our environment and circumstances for its expression" [*Body Code*, Lamb and Watson RKP 1979].

The test was run on 60 subjects who had been in their chosen careers for at least ten years to see if their Profiles bore a relation to their profession. The subjects were arranged in six groups according to profession with the following assumptions about the predominant category of behaviour to be found in people choosing that field of work:

- Accountants should be high in Investigating
- Inventors should be high in Exploring
- Barristers should be high in Determining
- Historians should be high in Evaluating
- Salespersons should be high in Timing
- Chess players should be high in Anticipating

The candidates were interviewed and the interviews were also videoed. The videos were then sent to "blind" [independent] observers who worked without sound and these observers' scores were used together with those given by a "blind" clerk for 47 results. The remaining 13 were given other tests.

Generally the original hypothesis that certain careers would be chosen by people with particular Action Profiles was proved, but with some additional unexpected results. It was found that whilst the majority of Inventors were indeed high in Exploring they were also good in Evaluating, Barristers were high in Timing as well as in Determining, and Salespersons in Investigating. Accountants who were strong in the Attention phase tended to stay longer in their profession than those who were strong in Commitment, the latter tending to use their skills in running their own companies.

Perhaps more importantly for Movement Analysis generally, the high correlation of all the results showed firstly that there was high inter-judge reliability, and secondly, because of the "blind" testing, that conversation has no impact on the results of movement observation analysis.

Du Nann's research therefore pointed to the reliability of Action Profiling and the significance of Posture-Gesture Merging, as well as the very significant reliability of the training of observers. But she was at pains to point to the need for further research in more aspects of the whole field of nonverbal communication. It was not clear, she claimed, how far the Action Profile might be measuring the process of translating thought into speech. If this were the case then the importance of language needs to be clarified. The fact that only trained observers could see PGMs proved to her that this was measuring cognitive and not social behaviour; in other words, that Action Profiling could get below any superficial behaviour. It could therefore be highly useful in an area otherwise beset by semantics and subjective opinion.

The problem then remained of the inaccessibility of the skills of observation. Profilers need a lengthy training of two but possibly five years, and the training is geared specifically to management consultancy, with much of it not relevant to the scientist. She concluded: "What other kinds of practical problems might be addressed with a tool which measures a deeply organised pattern of cognitive and movement style? These questions are far reaching, but so might be the implications of the central finding here: that human movement and thinking are tightly knit together, and that it is possible to measure the latter by closely observing the former."

Action Profiling had been reliably proved successful for industry both by controlled experiment and by years of use with top executives. On the other hand its potential for therapy, education and counselling whilst enormous, is still relatively undeveloped, particularly in Britain. In the United States Laban Movement Analysis has been used much more extensively, particularly in dance therapy. The potential of body movement to tell us more about learning styles, mental health, industrial health, methods of communication and many more aspects of human behaviour is relatively untapped. The ability to identify Integrated Movement would seem to be the ability to see the most alive and healthy part of human behaviour and sadly it is in the hands of relatively few people who [and this is not to criticise them] operate almost exclusively in business management or academia.

PROBLEMS FOR ACTION PROFILING INTERNATIONAL

All organisations in the end are the sum of their individual members, and API was no exception, despite its enormous skills at looking after its clients. Warren Lamb pleaded that they should use these skills to heal their own wounds, but to no avail. The unusual nature of the work, coming as it did out of an unorthodox background, made it always vulnerably attractive to fringe operators who would threaten the professionalism it so badly needed to preserve. As personality problems grew the standard of training of new Profilers became of increasing concern to Warren Lamb. The qualifying course was lengthy – as long as five years for most – but people would languish on it with no hope of ever qualifying whilst others might become members almost overnight. Concerns of this nature were already causing personality conflicts when more serious rifts brought matters to a head.

In his Presidential Address to the API Conference in 1986 Warren Lamb declared, "We are among the truest, most consistent and effective appliers of Laban's work ... Action Profiling incorporates the essence of Laban's genius." Again in December 1991, concluding his address to the Annual Conference of Action Profilers International in Colorado, he announced, "We are pure Laban". It was both a commendation and a warning, a shot across the bows to remind delegates what they were about, where their skills originated. He truly believed that Action Profiling was more closely descended from Laban's philosophy than any other work going on in Laban's name. Most other groups, whether in dance or therapy, had merged with other systems. Action Profiling still had the potential to stay "pure Laban".

In the same speech in 1991 he described Laban's legacy: "Much of what he taught is fragile, easily perverted, often misunderstood and even still is ahead of its time", and he reminded his audience of some of the themes which repeatedly occur in Laban's work:

- That we should always think in terms of movement
- That movement study should be guided by a set of principles and not translated into a system
- That harmony consists of the use of contrasts and opposites
- That body/mind unity is expressed in rhythm

The reminder of the origins of Action Profiling was timely. Warren Lamb found himself in an organisation inspired entirely by his development of Laban's work, but which he increasingly had to try to drag back on message. The temptation was always there for those around to seize on the Decision-Making Process or the Framework of Management Initiative, as fairly easy and useful concepts, and to devise systems for applying them without the preliminary movement analysis. Laban himself and Lawrence in 1952 had labelled their own selection process The Laban Lawrence Test, which Warren Lamb had to point out to them was the antithesis of Laban's own philosophy, fashionable though tests were at the time. A test implied failure, whereas to Laban who revered the uniqueness of the individual, no one's abilities were either good or bad, but only different.

Typical of this problem was a crisis in the mid-80s over a questionnaire. A candidate on Action Profile training sent a questionnaire he had devised to several members asking their opinion on it, and suggesting that this would be a useful and quicker way of initial selection, than the comparatively lengthy movement analysis, which could be reserved for short-listed candidates. The questionnaire was of course built round the Decision-Making Process. The person in question was himself a selection consultant called Michael Williams, who had invited a newly-trained Profiler to work for him, and had been enormously impressed by her work. He was a psychologist with experience of psychometric testing, and it was immediately apparent that he meant to use what he could of Action Profiling, but to turn it into something much easier to apply, even if that meant throwing out the movement observation and analysis. As Pamela Ramsden pointed out in a letter to all Action Profilers after the event, there was always a danger that someone would come along and pervert Action Profiling® by turning it into a psychometric test which would be quick, inexpensive and just accurate enough to sweep the board. It was tempting, and in fact Pamela Ramsden had demurred long enough for the situation to reach serious proportions.

In February 1989 the Council was forced to consider this matter of the "Management Decision Profile". The Council decided that he should not be allowed to use the name or logo of Action Profiling®, or the names of Warren Lamb or Pamela Ramsden in any of his marketing material. He accepted their decision and the affair was settled, but it was indicative of the type of problem which could so easily arise in an organisation of affiliated companies, each of which was largely autonomous.

In the May issue of *Action News* Warren Lamb gave his opinion and warnings on the matter. For him it seemed impossible that anyone without full training in movement observation should take the Framework and use it as though movement observation did not exist. That it could be applied independently of movement study was out of the question. He conceded only that there was a case for a Practitioner to use the Framework either to "supplement a properly made Action Profile, or simply to avoid the hassle of having to explain [to a client] how we take movement observations and translate them into a Profile". To use the Framework alone would be to reduce it to just one more of a big range of tests and questionnaires.

Even while this situation was developing and being resolved, another more serious issue was gradually unfolding between Warren Lamb and Pamela Ramsden.

The difficulties probably arose from a decision in 1984 of the Council of API to ask Pamela Ramsden to re-define polarities. The entire Framework of Management Initiative had been considerably developed and refined with ever more specific definitions. In their eagerness to make the system as accessible as possible for their clients, members were finding problems in easily explaining the meaning of the polarities. It was all part of the redefinition and clarification resulting from the elaboration of the theories on Sharing and Privacy in Interaction, which depended on understanding matching and mis-matching of the polarities. The polarities, it will be remembered, are the opposing qualities of the Shape, Effort and Flow continuums in the Decision Making Process. [Fig.12]

Pamela Ramsden produced new descriptions of the polarities which clearly defined the extremes, but which implied by their very lack of ambiguity that each polarity could stand alone. If a person's Profile contained Directing, for example, according to the new definition it would not of necessity contain Indirecting. Whereas Warren Lamb had expected the new definitions to be longer in order to be more explicit, those Pamela Ramsden had produced were short and simple. A person who was strong in Directing, for example, became a 'Prober', and a person strong in Indirecting became a 'Classifier'.

In his very earliest assessments of people at work Warren Lamb had included Development Possibilities in his reports. These generally referred to the possible reversal of a movement. He claimed that if a person showed a preference for movement with a particular quality, say towards Increasing Pressure, they were also capable of developing the opposite quality of Diminishing Pressure. If there were any movement in a range at all it would rate at least as a Development Possibility. Indeed to avoid paralysis some element of Diminishing Pressure however little, would already be evident.

To Pamela Ramsden the whole twelve polarities of the Decision Making Process could be simplified into 'types', with no confusing alternative possibilities [Fig.13]. To Warren Lamb this 'labelling' as he called it, could only neglect the essential 'see-saw' effect of movement, where each Effort or Shape has to some degree to be undone. A person with a propensity for Indirecting Attention must also potentially have Directing Attention otherwise their movement would become paralysed at the extreme of Indirecting. It is only as an intellectual exercise that the polarities can exist on their own. In movement terms they are notions joined by a continuum. The degree to which an individual 'undoes' movement is of equal sig-

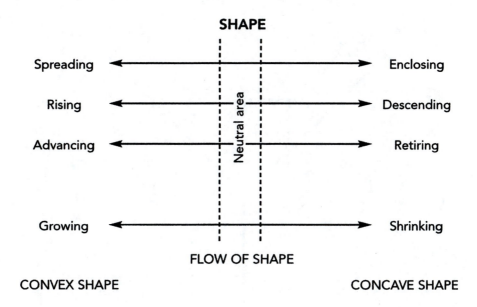

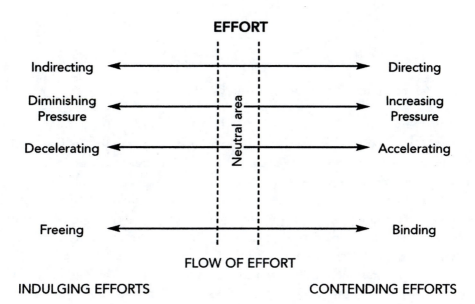

Fig. 12. Summary of Shape and Effort Graph

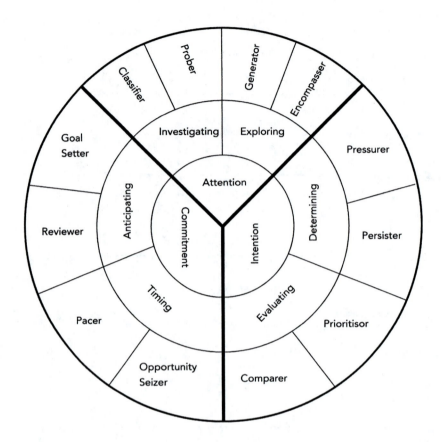

Fig. 13. A summary of the New Polarities devised by Pamela Ramsden

nificance in knowing the potential of the individual. To ignore the constant variation in movement seemed to Warren Lamb to be describing fixed positions, to
join the ranks of Body Language.

Pamela Ramsden's reply to these accusations was that when she spoke of
someone being high in a certain polarity she meant that their PGM showed a high
frequency geared to one side of the spectrum. But on returning from that end
of the spectrum, the movement would pass through 'neutral' – an indiscernible
area of movement, initiated by separate thought qualities. The movement may
not necessarily be at the extreme ends of the spectrum, but if this were the case
it would be useful to point out the tendency to an extreme to a client, so that
they could do something about it. Clients, she said, wanted results not to be told
about processes. The necessity to her was to give the client 'results, deliverables',

and making the polarities simpler was now more important than the subtleties of Laban's philosophy. It 'empowered' the client to make progress.

At first Warren Lamb tried to work with Pamela Ramsden's definitions of polarities, but eventually he had to voice his deep concerns and ask for them to be revised. Repeated discussions with Pamela Ramsden failed to achieve anything. She was not prepared to budge. The argument became a battle for the heart of API, an organisation which now regarded delivering a product to commercial clients as the priority. Warren Lamb's attempt to keep them true to Laban had failed.

The result was Warren Lamb's resignation as President of API, Chairman of the Council, and as a Member of Action Profilers International on October 31st 1992. In *Movement News* in Spring 1993 he described his action as traumatic and tragic, but necessary. He realised that it made the job of assessment much easier on the surface to use simplistic definitions. But he could not accept this trite perversion of the concept of movement analysis any more than he could see that in the long term the neat system which it had become, would give valid results. Lamb, like Laban before him, is against turning anything to do with movement into a "system". Movement is a constant process of variation, but Pamela Ramsden and the Practitioners who supported her were happy to talk about polarities as twelve different "items". At first glance it made their jobs both easier and quicker. But the entire either/or labelling actually created its own difficulties and in particular it made accurate PGM observations difficult.

Commercial considerations had inevitably triumphed however, and Warren Lamb reluctantly left the organisation he had inspired. He continues to work as hard as ever for his clients but has left behind the logo of Action Profiling® and now he and his colleagues call their work Movement Pattern Analysis. After fifty years he still has a remarkably pioneering attitude to movement study, eagerly pushing back the boundaries of what can be understood, and how it relates to other fields of human behavioural study.

Action Profiling International meanwhile continues but with only a handful of practitioners in the UK, USA and South Africa, each working from their own companies and using movement analysis as an adjunct to other selection systems and analysis techniques. All of this is of concern to Warren Lamb. It is probable, he knows, that the Decision-Making Process is itself being used on many occasions as a tool unfettered by the complication of having to carry out a movement analysis. An innovation in Action Profiling® is the extensive use of video, the reliability of which is again something about which Warren Lamb has always voiced his scepticism. A new category of Decision Adviser has also been created, requiring only the briefest two-day training. The Decision Adviser can then use video to record an interview and send the video to a qualified Action Profiler for analysis. The quality and reliability of an analysis made in this way is of course highly dependent on the number and positioning of the cameras for the video.

New profilers are still being trained. The amount of training required before qualification is fluid and the controls on its use are also less rigorous than Warren Lamb would find acceptable. The danger was always there however, that adaptations of movement analysis and the Decision-Making Process would eventually join the ranks of selection techniques as long as there are paying customers. The logo of Action Profiling® belongs to Action Profilers International who are responsible for its reputation.

CHAPTER SIX

MOVEMENT ANALYSIS AND PERSONALITY

CHILDHOOD DEVELOPMENT – JUDITH KESTENBERG

From the beginning of time people have read meaning into each other's behaviour at either a superficial or a sub-conscious level. Non-verbal behaviour was man's earliest means of communication, and its importance has been explored by scientists from many fields; Charles Darwin, Sigmund Freud and Margaret Mead to name a few. But Rudolf Laban stands alone. The sophisticated system of notation he devised meant that what was seen could be objectively, mathematically even, recorded and analysed. And from what he started Warren Lamb was able to arrive at the synthesis of individual movement, the Posture Gesture Merger.

Further validation of Laban and Lamb Movement Analysis is found in the work of Judith Kestenberg and Irmgard Bartenieff. Kestenberg was a Freudian child psychoanalyst from Vienna who moved to New York in the 1930s. She studied the rhythms of child behaviour, oral, anal and genital, and had a system of recording these as tension flow rhythms.

Through her work she came into contact in New York with Irmgard Bartenieff. Bartenieff had spent two years as a student of Laban's in Europe, after which she and her husband set up a dance school. Her husband was a Russian Jew, and it was propitious for them to emigrate to New York in the 1930s. They found America was not interested in the Central European dance they could offer, and Irmgard Bartenieff turned instead to physiotherapy. When she qualified two years later there was an outbreak of poliomyelitis. As a result she found her Laban training standing her in good stead as she introduced her patients to a much richer experience of movement than conventional physiotherapy could offer.

She later set up the Laban/Bartenieff Institute where she pioneered bodily therapy as an adjunct to the work of the emerging Dance Notation Bureau. It was Bartenieff who advised Kestenberg that her methodology would be improved by a study of Laban, and to this end for several years Kestenberg undertook training with Bartenieff and Warren Lamb. The influence of Laban through Warren Lamb on Kestenberg's work was immense. In thinking she moved away from the Freudian towards a more Jungian approach and she devised a system of notation based heavily on Labanotation to stand beside her tension flow notations.

The Kestenberg Movement Profile [KMP] was eventually formulated in the 1960s under the auspices of the Sands Point Study Group led by Judith Kestenberg. Their primary concern was with the mind/body relationship in child development, and with devising a tool for early detection of emotional problems particularly in child/parent relationships. Their work was supported by intensive research with children's schools and clinics in New York and Israel.

The resulting KMP closely reflects its strong Laban/Lamb influence, but with a broader base in psychology. It identifies 120 separate movement factors across 29 polar dimensions, and like Movement Pattern Analysis, it distinguishes between Effort and Shape. Effort it sees as concerned with the individual's perception of self [in Movement Analysis often referred to as assertion], and it is divided into 4 four qualities. Shape [in Movement Analysis often called perspective] it sees as related to one's relationship to people and things. A further graph relates to Body Attitude. Both Effort and Shape have polarities bearing a close resemblance again to Movement Analysis.

Effort	Shaping in Planes
Indirect ——————— Direct	Spreading ——————— Enclosing
Lightness ——————— Strength	Ascending ————— Descending
Deceleration ——— Acceleration	Advancing ——————— Retreating

In many other ways there are similarities between the two systems. For example Laban's 8 Basic Efforts can be compared with the KMP ten rhythmic patterns: sucking, biting, twisting, straining, running, stopping/starting, undulating, swaying, jumping, and leaping. KMP, like Movement Pattern Analysis, also concerns itself with the desirability of affinities between Effort and Shape, both in the individual and between child and parent.

According to KMP, each aspect of Effort and Shape identified in the nine charts develops during infancy, even from pre-birth. How they show in our movement as adults will depend on how each one has been allowed to develop, or how far they have been arrested by, for example, trauma or over-disciplining. In normal development, it claims, the child will progress from:

[1] the horizontal lying in its cot, stretching, widening and narrowing with its limbs to

[2] the vertical phase when it gradually gets to its feet, learning to balance in a squatting position before pushing up to standing, to

[3] walking and propulsion.

To pass through all these phases requires a huge exercise in learning and experimentation with muscle control, mobility and stability. The way in which this development takes place is fundamental to the formation of personality and in turn is demonstrated by the eventual movement pattern of the adult. KMP therefore offers an explanation of how the adult movement pattern analysed by Lamb is formed.

A summary of such a finely detailed system cannot do it justice, and can only be undertaken with the proviso that it is incomplete and deals only with those aspects bearing a direct correlation to Movement Analysis. Given this proviso, a summary of the three main areas of movement development offers an interesting explanation of how adults develop their individuality in the three stages of the Decision-Making Process identified by Warren Lamb.

1. **The Horizontal Phase**

   In the first year the infant does a lot of spreading and enclosing, widening and narrowing movements. These are related to establishing communication, giving and receiving attention, and exploring the environment. They do not necessarily relate to seeking food and protection. The development of a balance of movement between spreading and enclosing reflects an ability to give and take, to accept or refuse. These abilities will relate later in life to seeking out new ideas and consolidating on information, to making new friends but valuing the old. An imbalance in this area of movement would indicate a lack of discrimination, welcoming everyone but remembering no one's name, and at the same time making loved ones feel insecure.

2. **The Vertical Dimension**

   This is related by Kestenberg to the second year of life, when a child most commonly literally gets to its feet. Movements in this plane are described as being concerned with intentionality, presentation, evaluation and confrontation. It is a time to develop the notion of "standing one's ground" as well as the related values of discovering shame. Distress and despair are also associated with downward movements, just as elation and joy are with upward movement. Descending with strength [increasing pressure] commands authority, whereas ascending, "drawing oneself up to full height", is connected with presenting, confronting and inspiring others. Children going through this phase can easily get irrationally locked into an attitude, giving rise to the 'terrible twos' with their screaming tantrums.

3. **The Sagittal Plane**

   Developed in the third year of life, this phase reflects the development of ideas of anticipation, decision-making and commitment to operation. On the one hand it contains retreating action, seeking security in the past or nostalgia, or alternatively a tactical withdrawing to get a better view of the situation before taking action. The opposite Advancing shape – rather blowing oneself out – is connected with initiating action and can be aggressive in appearance. If it is not balanced by sufficient retreating it can indicate the over-achiever, or taking decisions with no regard for what has gone before. Children at three are liable to run away from their carers, which does not necessarily mean they are unhappy, but rather that they simply want to experiment with this behaviour. They also favour pushy-pully toys. The person who combines advancing with deceleration is a person who will move forward with deliberation and care, whereas it is easy to imagine that the person who combines it with acceleration may be going headlong into disaster.

These phases lay down the groundwork for the development of behaviour in the growing child. In any three year old there is still a large percentage of Flow in their movement and their behaviour pattern will continue to develop until well into their teens. Parents, teachers and friends will all impact on the final ratio of movement, but the Kestenberg analysis of early development is interesting in describing the way our approach to Decision Making is formed from the cradle. The sum total of influences and experiences determine the final outcome and to illustrate this let us take a simple example from everyday life.

We have all at some time in our lives grimaced at the way other people bring up their children. Imagine a mother with her young son in a toy shop. The child has to choose which toy to buy with his pocket money and the mother has various options in handling this simple situation. Does she say: "Now, Johnny, you walk around and take a good look at everything. Don't let anyone hurry you, just make sure you look at everything." The whole world must wait for her child to do his exploration of the toyshop, but the child is at least being given time to carry out this task for himself. Hopefully she will also be ready to give some guidance in choosing, drawing his attention to this or that feature of a toy. If she doesn't he may find it all too much to cope with and finally just snatch at something.

Or does she say, "Look at this. Do you see how much it costs? Can you guess how long it will last? Is it educational, fashionable, damaged, pretty, etc. etc?" He has been rushed through the exploratory stage straight into a morass of pros and cons about one isolated toy. He is also being encouraged to take a decision based only on hand-me-down opinions.

Alternatively the mother's approach may be: "Why don't you buy this? This is what you should have. We can't spend all day here and there are people waiting so do hurry." The mother with her greater knowledge and experience is sure she knows what the child would ultimately choose if allowed to, and can see no point in wasting time while he gets there himself. The child is therefore rushed straight through to a commitment without a moment's reflection on the possibilities.

The totality of incidents like this starting from birth make up the experience and also the movement pattern of the growing individual. To the child the physical behaviour of the mother, parent, guardian or carer, will be as important as what they actually say. Sadly in the real, rushed world most of us live in, the last option is probably the most common, but many situations are an amalgam of these extremes. Today's demands on children to perform at school and compete socially mean they are increasingly hurtled through life from one experience to another. School life begins at a younger and younger age, with Homework Policies now for five year olds. Some are even advocating educating children in the womb! From infancy there seems to be less and less priority placed on the need to enable children to discover the world for themselves in a caring, secure environment and to make it fun.

The emphasis is on packaged entertainment and education. Is it any wonder that when children do have time to themselves they can only spend it prone in front of a screen, blotting out the pressures of their lives perhaps with limited ability to explore and make their own entertainment? The process of growing-up in such a competitive busy world can too easily leave children without any skills for structuring their own lives and enjoyably occupying themselves. Parents, too, are often preoccupied achievers, anxious to live their own lives and with only a dubious commodity called "quality time" to give their children.

Both Kestenberg and Lamb agree that the early years are critically important in the formation of personality and that the results are demonstrated in our physical behaviour, which in itself is a reflection of the cognitive process. They agree also on the three main stages of thought, to Lamb the Decision Making Process, which each person approaches in their distinctly individual way. This thought process is reflected in a movement pattern which in itself is a reflection of the individual's character and abilities.

SOME BASIC PERSONALITY TYPES – CARDBOARD CUT-OUTS

Putting together the theories of Kestenberg and Lamb on personality development and its manifestation in non-verbal behaviour, three basic personality types can be identified according to their strengths in each phase of the Decision Making Process. To imagine that three types truly exist in their purest form is of course a nonsense. People are much more complicated than these cardboard cut-outs. Like the crystal forms studied by Laban, people are multi-faceted. But for simplicity – and fun – we can imagine three basic types against which to compare our behaviour.

These "types" would have to have perfect affinity between Shape and Effort in each of the three ranges, with one range clearly dominant over the other two ranges. Few people would have such a clear dominance of one range of behaviour over the others, and even more unlikely is it that each would be perfectly balanced as well as having affinity between Effort and Shape. Everyone is made up of different proportions of each and with preponderances toward one end of a range or another. But for present purposes let us imagine that we have three such perfectly balanced characters, each with one predominant range of behaviour. Let us call them The Communicator, The Confronter and Action Man or Woman.

1. The **Communicator** would predominate in the Horizontal range of Shape and the Space range in Effort. Main characteristics: Broadly observant, exploratory, attentive to others, a good listener, difficult to surprise, clarity of exposition. His or her graphs would look like this:

	Attention	
	Intention	
	Commitment	
SHAPE		EFFORT

Fig. 14.

2. The **Confronter** would predominate in the Vertical range of Shape and in the Pressure range of Effort. Main characteristics: Forceful, determined; easy expression of authority; often dedicated; always clear where he/she stands. His or her graphs would look like this:

	Attention	
———————	Attention	———————
——————————————	Intention	——————————————
———————	Commitment	———————

| SHAPE | EFFORT |

Fig. 15.

3. **Action Man/Woman** has a well-developed Sagittal range of Shape and is strong in the Time range of Effort. Main characteristics: Decisive, always appears ready for action; facility in carrying through a programme; planning and organising ability; naturally systematic. His or her graphs look like this:

	Attention	
———————	Attention	———————
———————	Intention	———————
——————————————	Commitment	——————————————

| SHAPE | EFFORT |

Fig. 16.

The predominant personality characteristics of these three types are so different that confronted with an identical situation they would each take a completely different course of action, and the outcome for everyone affected would be quite different. This was demonstrated in experiments carried out for Action Profiling® [Chapter Five].

Let us imagine two situations, one at work and the other at home. A sales director in a medium-sized company has received an unfavourable report on an area salesman. At home a father has received a poor end-of-term report on his son. [For simplicity of writing the characters are all male, but personality types are certainly not gender based.]

1. The Communicator:

The person whose preponderance is to Horizontal Spreading/Enclosing movements and Directing/Indirecting Efforts, is constantly looking around, taking in the components of his environment in a general way and [given the perfect balance between the polarities we are here assuming] he pays equally close attention to detail. He likes to browse and investigate. This person will seek to know everything to do with the report in front of him. On discovering the bad sales figures of his subordinate, or the poor exam results of his child, he will then spend hours, perhaps days, looking into the facts of the case. He will seek information from others to "get the whole picture", and will most likely collect more information than can possibly be necessary. Some of it may not even be helpful. His "exploring" is equally matched [in our prototype] with close investigation for the detailed as well as the general picture. No stone is left unturned.

In all this activity he will have been in touch with a great number of people, collecting information and probably spreading information from one to the other. How far he does this, however, depends on another aspect of the behavioural equation – Affinity. With his high degree of Affinity between Shape and Effort he will truly communicate as he proceeds with his data collection, without much Affinity it becomes a private activity.

Our Communicator will be seen as a "great guy" – accessible and easy to talk to, a friend to everyone, a source of endless anecdotes. But will he do anything with this information – there's the rub. He may eventually write a lengthy letter to the salesman, criticising and cajoling, but will not, left to his own devices, call him in for a dressing-down. Similarly he may find it impossible to deal sternly and effectively with the school child, even though he is aware of the need for action. Whilst our Communicator has been deeply affected by the sales figures and the school report therefore, he has not necessarily done anything to alter the behaviour of either the salesman or his son.

2. The Confronter:

The Sales Director or parent whose predominant movement is in the Vertical Plane of Shape and the Pressure range of Effort will be more than willing to confront the salesman or the school child, and to deliver whatever ultimatum or reprimand may be necessary. They will be in no doubt as to "where he stands" on the matter, or what values he represents. His Shaping is in a "Here I am!" way, and is either full of stern authority or haughtily rising above the situation in a manner designed to make the culprit feel demeaned. His Effort will reinforce this with either downward pressure and "laying-down-the-law", or with a gentleness of touch which again is humbling to the culprit. As parents or schoolteachers, such people can be fearsome without raising a finger, arousing either admiration and feelings of allegiance, or shame in those they confront. How well-founded their opinions are is another matter, and depends heavily on the quality of information fed to them, since they are not inclined to spend much energy finding things out for themselves.

Furthermore their method of taking action is based on adopting an attitude, but may not go very far in terms of actually doing anything more about it. If the salesman or the schoolchild can ride out the storm, they may find no sanctions have actually been placed on them. Again the degree of Affinity in our Confronter will also determine how far others are brought into the situation. Does he fume in private while others creep around giving him a wide berth, or does he storm out of his office, noisily demanding the salesman/school child present themselves immediately?

The tendency of the media today is to take an Intention based stance, encouraging an immediate attitude to objects and situations either directly or by implication. The message contains both the implication that indisputable research has produced this argument, and also a hidden exhortation to action.

"Nine out of ten scientists agree on the dangers of ..."
"Illegal immigrants over-run..."
"Hair looks silkier with shampoo by ..."

Readers are encouraged into a stance based on minimal selected 'facts', which are carefully presented and packaged to ensure the reader stays on message. In an information drenched age of global communication processed attitudes can be irresistible. Unfortunately they slide down as easily and have as many health risks as junk food, and the artificial stimulants they contain can equally lead to hyperactivity and confrontation.

3. Action Man:

The final stage in the decision making process is the area of Sagittal Shape and Timed Effort. It is the stage of behaviour associated with taking action. The person who is low on attention-giving or intention-forming but high in commitment can obviously be a walking disaster, an undirected exocet missile. On hearing the bad sales figures or reading the poor school report, he will rush into action.

The salesman will be sacked, the schoolchild will be sent to his room, deprived of pocket-money, taken out of school.

The reports may, of course, point towards some other culprit – faulty products, poor teaching – in which case the exocet will point himself in that direction. How effective or how justified his action is will depend heavily on the quality of information presented to him and how far it is slanted one way or the other. He is a sucker for banner headlines and sound-bites, having little inclination to find or evaluate information for himself.

On the other hand, something gets done, and one can only hope it is to improve things and not the reverse. These can be people who effect change by the excellence of their timing. They can be sensitive actors, great comedians, astute politicians, natural sportsmen. They thrive in situations requiring results.

It is fun to type ourselves and analyse our friends, whether by graphology, astrology or simply by the cut of a person's clothes. We do it all the time, especially with strangers, in order to cope with the world, to sort people out. The verbal games we play when we meet new people are accompanied by physical posturing – unconscious or otherwise – that are a substitution for the physical stand-offs of primitive people and animals. We are making a first line assessment of what sort of person they are – are they 'our sort of person' or not, are they a threat, will they be interesting or fun, socially advantageous to know? We grade them and type them according to the information available to us. In totally unfamiliar surroundings we may at first be all at sea, trying to find some distinguishing features to separate one person from the other, sometimes making completely foolish judgements because we have brought the wrong criteria to the situation. The less confident we are the harder we will try to make our judgements. For most people it is all rather hit and miss.

The Decision-Making Process – Attention, Intention, Commitment – can be a useful way of thinking through our behaviour or that of our acquaintances. It enables us to define the various stages of ours and other people's approach to a situation, and to analyse our way of working through them. Without being able to observe and notate movement it can perhaps provide an organised way of working out what is going on. But without notation it can also be as flawed as any other system depending as it does on the subjective perception of the observer. This may be with the help of carefully planned questions, but even so the interviewer has no reliable way of eliminating his or her own subjectivity, or of seeing through contrivance on the part of the person being assessed.

This is especially the case in the average interview – possibly the bluntest instrument for personnel selection and yet strangely the most common. No one would dream of appointing a person totally from paper evidence of qualifications. There is a real need to experience what it is like to be with a person, to see the 'cut of his jib', and yet how many interviewers really know what they are seeing? Supposing the candidate's answers consistently refer to the need for decisiveness and timing, is this because he/she is strong in this area, or is it conversely because their weakness in that direction is a worry to them? Perhaps he/she simply decided on the way to the interview that decisiveness would impress and every opportunity should be taken to demonstrate it by their answers. The interviewer will in the end have to use his or her own intuition to decide whether this decisiveness rang true. In other words was it backed up by their physical behaviour? Some people are highly sensitive and intuitive, but for most of us our judgement is largely based upon an amalgam of personal and social prejudices.

CHAPTER SEVEN

MOVEMENT AND GENDER

The history of the development of Movement Analysis from its seeds in Laban's folk dances and mass pageants, through to the sophistication of Action Profiling can be fitted conveniently along a continuum, in which to a large degree one thing progresses from another. This is far from the whole story of course. Other applications of movement observation run alongside this, occasionally feeding into it and at other times drawing from it. The work done by therapists such as Bartenieff and Kestenberg is a case in point, as is the regular and active connection between Warren Lamb, the theatre and modern dance both in England and North America. Seminars and conferences in both countries continually examine the many possible applications of movement analysis and a recurring subject throughout the last three decades has been that of movement and gender.

To suggest that men and women really are different and in a way which means they are suited to different occupations, is as dangerous as walking on eggs. The area is as emotionally charged as it is complex. But it may be worthwhile for Movement Analysis to 'throw its hat into the ring' if doing so will provide any clarification of the male/female condition. It is in any case a fascinating aspect of movement and one Warren Lamb explores frequently with drama and dance pupils.

THE GENDER WAR

Western society is still in a state of confusion over the proper role of women. Attitudes remain polarized between those "traditionalists" who believe a "woman's place is in the home", and those who believe that careers, housework and children are completely joint rights or responsibilities of the sexes. Most people fluctuate somewhere in the middle, but sadly both standpoints start from the premise that running a home and caring for a family is a low value occupation within the capabilities of anyone. Not true. It is one of the most difficult jobs on earth to do well, and there are plenty of casualties of poorly run homes at every level of society.

In fact there is nothing traditional about women managing the home single-handed and men going out to work. It is a fairly recent innovation of urban society created probably by centres of work being far from home instead of on the doorstep. There is no basis biologically, economically or socially for believing that this is a "natural" arrangement, as a cursory look into anthropology will prove. In most societies child-rearing and bringing home the bacon are shared activities, and importantly, with equal values. What is life about after all but providing food and shelter and propagating the species?

Sometime early in the 20th Century our society arrived at a point where everything a woman does is regarded as having less status than man's work. Nurturing children and their early education, predominantly the domain of women, is pitifully paid. "Men's work" is more highly valued, whether that be manufacturing or selling arms, cigarettes or motorcars, or the countless jobs in offices and management people do every day but which have zero impact on the course of history. It became truly a man's world, and it was inevitable the balance would have to be redressed.

As the balance swung the other way 'women's rights' have become of paramount consideration. As happens with all types of discrimination, when it is reversed the pendulum goes for a while too far in the opposite direction. Pinching a woman's bottom at a drunken office party is now a sackable offence for a man, but it is unlikely that a woman would be sacked for such an impropriety against a man.

But women's "liberation" has proved to be a bit of a Hobson's Choice. The old attitudes hang on by a slender persistent thread in the minds of many women just as much as they do in the minds of men, and "having it all" has proved to be no liberation at all, involving as it does for most women an incredible juggling act between work/home/husband/children. Then again there are those women who, for whatever reason, do not have all of these responsibilities but are put on the defensive about being either career-less or childless. Looked at in this way it sometimes seems that men have been liberated more than women.

The balmy days when a woman could get married and put her feet up are vanishing fast. Now she is a signatory to the mortgage. Conversely a young man contemplating marriage no longer needs to feel anxiety that he will be the sole breadwinner and will have several uninterrupted decades of meeting all the household expenses. He can take a much more relaxed view about his career and his pension rights than he could before.

Whatever the reason it is evident that there is still confusion in the minds of many, an ambivalence about what is, if there is such a thing, the fair relationship at home and at work between men and women. In the best cases – unpublicised of course – economic necessity and caring, civilised behaviour determine who does what to earn the money and run the home. In others there is gross unfairness of one party to another. The world was ever thus. There will always be some people who are naturally thoughtless and unkind.

At work it seems it is easier for men to move into women's professions – secretarial, nursing – than for women to move into men's territory – the senior ranks of the armed forces for example. The Clinton administration was eager to promote the "gentler sex" in the armed forces, bringing their numbers up from 12% to 20% in a decade, and the result has been a mayhem of dismissals for immoral behaviour and cases of sexual harassment. The battle fairly typically is between the brass hats who are hell bent on denying women access to senior positions in the armed services, and the radical feminists who lay down ludicrous rules about, for example, how long a glance at a woman can be before it becomes sexual harassment. Similarly in Britain cases of harassment and discrimination abound particularly in the finance industry, and are eagerly taken up by the press, all of which must have a negative effect on the careers of those women who simply want to get on with the job and earn a good living.

The clash seems to be on two main fronts. Men feel threatened by women moving in on their territory; and both sides bring old and inappropriate gender attitudes to their new work situation. Without recourse to the law, women are more likely to be the losers in both battles. Take politics as an example. "Disgraced" men politicians can be accused of bisexuality, promiscuity, incompetence, even lying and dubious financial practice yet still bounce back into public life at a later date. Once a woman is out there is normally no way back, even though her failings or 'misdemeanours' were slight. As Northern Ireland Secretary in Britain in the 1990s, Mo Mowlam had enormous success in this sensitive post and was dearly loved there, but was never acceptable to the diehard Ulstermen. For the peace process to move forward she was not only sacrificed but sidelined completely by a male whispering campaign and decided to give up politics. Baroness Thatcher steered her party from victory to victory and yet many of those who rode on her coat-tails complained throughout of being "handbagged", and were like rats off a sinking ship at her demise. Women have to be so much better than men to survive in politics, and still have to have eyes in the back of their heads to watch out for the knives.

Why is a career-minded woman called hard when a man is tough, or aggressive when a man is dynamic? A man can be good on detail, but a woman will be regarded as nit-picking, a man can be vehement when a woman is thought hysterical; he can be authoritative, but she can be power-mad. In social life it is the same. A promiscuous man is a "Bit of Don Juan" who "likes the ladies", whilst a woman who flaunts her sexuality even flirtatiously is a Scarlet Woman who "sleeps around". A man who drinks is one of the boys, but a woman is fallen, and so it goes on. Men regularly run round with their shirts over their heads after scoring in a football match. But when Brandi Chastain did so after scoring the winning goal in the1999 Fifa World Cup, an almighty storm erupted about the indecency of the act. Brandi was actually wearing a sports bra much more substantial and more modest than any bikini top, so what was it that made people find her action so alarming?

The truth is that it is still a man's world. For whatever reason, every study shows that women still do most of the housework, even when they go out to work for the same hours as their partners. Men still fix the shelves and the car, then go to the pub while the wife cooks lunch or babysits the children, and if they are given parental leave the chances are most of it will be spent on the golf course rather than rocking the cradle. The strident calls of feminism and the counter claims of men have solved little in comparison with the time-consuming, unproductive distress created, fuelled by eager lawyers and newspaper barons. Issues relating to gender have never been far from the front pages in recent years. Courts have been inundated with hugely expensive cases, most of which would have been regarded as laughable thirty years ago.

The evolution of a proportion of women to more serious careers would probably have taken place anyway, driven by market forces as a by-product of social changes: education, two world wars and household gadgetry to name a few contributors. The consequent gradual re-division of household tasks with men going to the supermarket [because they love it!] and having a greater involvement with the children's upbringing [because they have more leisure time], would also have taken place. It may even be that militancy on either side has made a natural process so much more painful. It has certainly taken a lot of fun out of life.

THE MALE AND FEMALE IN MOVEMENT

"Hobbs's information that men do twice as much work as girls is exaggerated", wrote Laban in 1943 after making observations at Dartington sawmills, where Hobbs presumably was a manager. "Objectively the work movements of trained girls are not only different but also better than those of apparently skilled men." Such a remark would cause much more interest today than it did then. One can imagine the tabloid headline: "Girls are better workers than Men – Fact!" But that would be to miss the crucial truth of what he was saying: that in performing the same tasks women's movements were "different". Whatever the task in the sawmills Laban was teaching them to do more efficiently and with less stress, the girls had shown more aptitude for it than the men.

Lamb recalls that in his dance classes Laban taught that men do 'strong' movements and women 'light'. He would need to do so, of course, to create an easily understood dramatic effect, to tell a story to the audience. In industry during the war on the other hand, Laban proved that men and women could do the same work equally well, that they could both exercise strength or delicacy, but that they had to do the same job in a different way. The difference he understood was only partly one of physique and musculature. In those days before the Gender War began, it was not a difference Laban found it necessary to pursue. In these more "gender sensitive" times, however, the difference has increasingly preoccupied and interested Warren Lamb.

Part of the answer must lie in what Warren Lamb has found to be the difference in the way men and women phrase their movement, so that when they are behaving similarly or performing the same task with the same result, the perception of what they are about is quite different. These differences he has always found to be cross-cultural, regardless of widely differing roles of men and women in different parts of the world. Whether this results from the practical exigencies of human evolution and qualities of male/female physique is not relevant in this context. To analyse that may explain but would not offer any solutions for modern society. But it is important to recognise that a difference exists, and that perhaps movement analysis can explain what is happening. Understanding may itself point the way to coping with this area of controversy in modern life.

Previous chapters have shown that a person's individual movement pattern reveals a great deal about their personality and their work aptitudes. The reliability of this in the hands of skilled observers has been proved both by years of practical application and by research in the field. If the same observers then find fundamental differences between male and female movement patterning, it is encouraging to believe this must have a significance for us in considering gender at work and in society.

Thousands of randomly selected observations were recorded in Europe, North America, Africa, India and South East Asia, of men and women in streets, restaurants and other public places. It is not claimed here that this was a clinically controlled piece of research, but what validation was possible was carried out and the results indicate that it is an area worthy of greater study.

THE IMPORTANCE OF FLOW – AGAIN

The focus for the researchers in fact became the manner in which men and women use Effort Flow and Shape Flow, and how they combine these with the twelve polarities of Effort and Shape. The fundamental discovery was that men and women combine Flow with the polarities of Effort and Shape in exactly the opposite ways from each other. Men make an affinity between their use of Effort Flow and Effort; that is they combine Freeing Effort Flow with the Indulging polarities of Effort and Binding Effort Flow with the Contending polarities. Women do the opposite; they combine Freeing Effort Flow with Contending Effort and Binding Effort Flow with the Indulging Effort polarities. The combinations are shown on the chart [Fig.17].

A man's Freeing Effort Flow, combined as it is with the Indulging Efforts of Indirecting, Diminishing Pressure and Decelerating will therefore make his behaviour look "laid back" and relaxed. A woman exercising Freeing Effort Flow will combine it with the Contending Efforts of Directing, Increasing Pressure and Accelerating and this will make her look eager to act and get on with things.

To give an initial example, imagine a woman exercising Freeing Effort Flow and combining this as she would with Contending Effort. She may be whirling about in a busy, bustling way doing all the things mothers have to do to get the children out to school in the morning. She appears unstoppable, driven, with her focussed Effort and rapid stringing together of movements. A man trying to do her job in the morning will look quite different. If he uses Freeing Effort Flow his Effort will be on the Indulging side, he will be relaxed to such a point the children will be anxious about getting to school on time. If he does the opposite and uses Contending Effort together with Binding Effort Flow he will become scary, a sergeant major.

When it comes to Shape Flow the sexes again do exactly the opposite. Women combine Growing Shape Flow with its Convex affinities of Spreading, Rising and Advancing – creating the impression that when they are having a good time they are really going to let their hair down. But men combine Growing Shape Flow with the opposite, Concave, polarities of Enclosing, Descending and Retiring, and give a more careful appearance to their expansive behaviour. The combinations again are more easily understood by referring to the chart.

The various possible combinations can be summarised as follows:

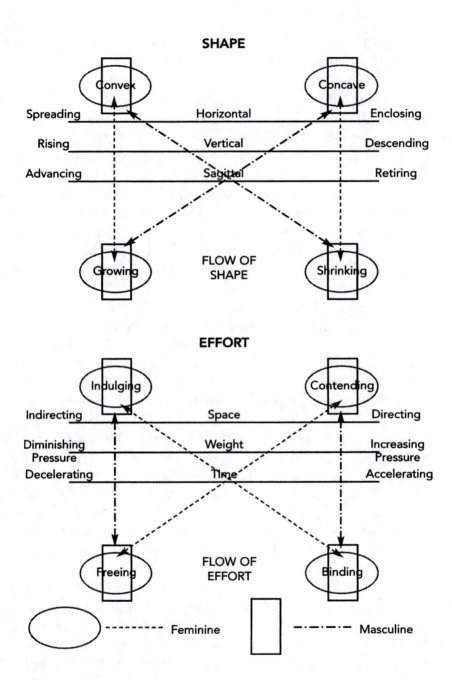

Fig. 17. Male and Female Preferences in Movement Patterning © Warren Lamb

1. Women associate Growing Shape Flow with Spreading, Rising and Advancing postural movements. In a mood to Grow they will look their most loosely relaxed and open, but also by Growing they can become more vulnerable.
2. Men associate Growing Shape Flow with Enclosing, Descending and Retiring postural movements. When they Grow they make themselves look self-protective, assertive and authoritative.
3. Women associate Shrinking Shape Flow with Enclosing, Descending and Retiring postural movements, all the notions associated with care and attention to a restricted area, the archetypal protective carer.
4. Men associate Shrinking Shape Flow with Spreading, Rising and Advancing postural movements. When in charge of a small area they are ready to defend it, are on the look-out for friend or foe.
5. Women associate Freeing Flow of Effort with Directing [focussing] and Accelerating qualities of movement and Increasing Pressure. In this aspect when a woman sees what has to be done she is all action and gets on with it.
6. Men associate Freeing Flow of Effort with Indirecting and Decelerating qualities of movement and Diminishing Pressure. A man seeing what has to be done first takes a bit of time looking around, talking around the subject with friends and colleagues. Perhaps he will take note of all the committees and procedures to be gone through.
7. Women associate Binding Flow of Effort with Indirecting, Decreasing Pressure and Decelerating qualities of movement. Women may use Binding Flow of Effort for caution when they are anxious to avoid and delay action.
8. Men associate Binding Flow of Effort with Directing, Increasing Pressure and Accelerating qualities of movement. Their Binding Flow of Effort is a sign of confidence, meaning they will get on with the job.

SOME INTERPRETATIONS

In Chapter Three Choreutics (here known as Shape) was described as the architectural or sculptural aspect of movement, the fundamental demonstration of how we feel about ourselves. Eukinetics (or Effort) was described as the intensity or nature of the activity put into movement according to how we feel about our environment. It is worth reflecting now on what this means for the behaviour of each sex, at a time when there is a lot of talk about equality, if female behaviour makes the affinities and is stronger in Shape, and male behaviour by using the affinities is stronger in Effort.

It has to be emphasised all along that the differences in male and female patterning are tendencies only. Not all men have all male patterning any more than all women have all female patterning, but most members of each sex display for the greater part the appropriate patterning. In Shaping our movement we close off from that we find hostile and open up to things we deem friendly, we show the world our nature, whether communicative or aloof, bold or shy. Feminine behaviour is therefore more attuned to the emotional, intuitive and personal aspects of life.

Our Effort on the other hand represents the mark we want to make on our environment, the change we wish or do not wish to make whether in terms of space, weight or time. With Contending Effort combined with Binding Flow of Effort, a man's investigative skills will not be curbed by sensitivities as those of a woman's would tend to be, and a punch will be delivered full force. In a woman whose assertive Effort is neutralised to some degree by its combination with Freeing Flow of Effort, to achieve the same result she will naturally take a less direct and perhaps more intuitive route to achieve the same result. There is a fundamental difference in the behaviour of the sexes, and try as they might, they will surely always have their separate ways of approaching life.

Following the arrows on the chart (page 116), consider the use of Shape Flow, and what it means for a woman if as she Grows, she combines this with the Convex Shaping. She has made herself open and highly visible, even vulnerable. She has confidently walked into a room and is an immediate target for whatever attitudes that room contains, good or bad, favourable or unfavourable. If she wants to make a less assertive entry she will take the method of folding her arms across her, perhaps in the guise of clutching a bag, and adopt a more 'Shrinking' attitude.

Compare this with the man who when he Grows to make himself as big as possible combines this with a Concave Shape, for example by folding his arms or crossing his legs. In making himself appear bigger, he has also acted to protect himself. When he walks confidently into a crowded room he will take a hand across to straighten his tie, and bring his shoulders forward slightly, or pull the edges of his jacket together. It surely indicates something about the social behaviour of men and women – perhaps that when women feel confident they will "grow" in a very open way, whereas men are always more cautious and protective about doing so.

To consider now Shrinking Shape Flow, a man combines this with the Convex aspects of Shape, so that although he "Shrinks" he adopts a more aggressive, assertive posture. He might be 'defending his corner'. In this sense a man's behaviour is always taking account of his environment, in that he is either defensively or aggressively arranging his behaviour to meet the world. A man naturally wants to have some relationship with what is going on around him. The female tendency on the other hand of patterning the affinities of Shape Flow and Shape together make her very open to society when using Growing Shape Flow, but quite closed off from society when using Shrinking Shape Flow.

A woman holding a baby will cuddle it to her [Concave Shaping] and at the same time she "Shrinks" and makes her world smaller. Her attitude is, "My baby and I are occupying our own little world; don't disturb us." Isn't that just what young wives are warned about when a new baby arrives – the danger of looking so wrapped up in the child that their husbands feel left out? A man, on the other hand, will make the same Enclosing movement to hold the baby, but will combine this with Growing his kinesphere, as if to say "Look what I've got!" showing the baby off, or perhaps while holding it he is also keeping a protective lookout.

To turn now to an example of the use of Effort Flow, we have said that men combine Binding Flow of Effort with Contending Effort. This enables a man walking along a mountain ledge, a railway line or a tightrope to naturally both direct his feet precisely and control his movement. It is less easy for a woman to do this since her natural tendency is to make the opposite patterning of Freeing Flow of Effort with Contending Effort, and Binding Flow of Effort with Indulging Effort. She will find it more difficult and more strain to do any of these activities. Whilst Directing [her feet on the narrow path or wire] her tendency is to swing freely along. To exercise the necessary Binding Flow of Effort she would then want to indulge in stepping out more casually than the situation permits.

There is no physical reason why the sexes should not use the polarities in exactly the same way, but according to Warren Lamb, the combination of Binding Flow of Effort with Directing is more often seen in a man, and comes more naturally to the male sex. It may explain why men are more often seen as tightrope walkers than women, because instinctively when they have to apply the Directing Effort required for walking on a tightrope they link it with Binding Flow of Effort. This is not to suggest that a woman cannot be a tightrope walker – many are – but the skill does seem to come more easily to a man. Acrobatic horse-back riding, the way women do it, makes the natural combination of Freeing Flow of Effort with Contending Effort very successfully so that it is graceful as well as being controlled. A man's performance usually looks much more strongly controlled throughout. Compare also how men and women trapeze artists move differently during their act, including their initial run up to the rope, or the difference

in performance between male and female ballet dancers. What is perceived as 'feminine' is the graceful [Freeing] flow of women's movement compared with the more athletic, controlled [Binding] movement of the man.

A knowledge of the distinction in male/female use of Flow may have been helpful to researchers at the University of Alabama into handshaking. Four shakers or "coders" were instructed for a month in how to de-code handshakes, and shook the hands of 112 students ostensibly as a greeting when they came to do personality tests. The research sought to establish whether a handshake is a true reflection of personality. On the whole men had firmer handshakes than women because they were assertive and expressive and also used eye-contact. When women gave a "male" handshake they gave a much better impression to others than when they used their more usual weak handshake. What confounded the researchers was that women with a firm handshake were open and liberal, but when a man was open and liberal he had a weak handshake. No doubt the liberal women were combining their Freeing Effort Flow with Contending Effort to produce a firm handshake, whilst the liberal men were combining it with Indulging Effort, hence the 'wet fish' handshake. It's so simple when you know!

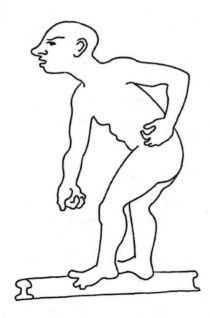

Binding Flow of Effort + Contending Effort. A man walking on a railway line

Growing one's personal kinesphere – making oneself bigger – is most naturally associated with attitudes of dominance, pride, expressions of confidence, outgoingness, extraversion, all of which can be expressed by both men and women. In the West confidence and outgoingness are the most common prerequisites of success in either sex. If a woman wants to be successful she must in some way assert herself. Will this be by Growing her Shape and thus making herself more vulnerable by being also more open, or will it be by Freeing Flow of Effort combined with Contending Effort, leaving "no stone unturned" in her progress to the top? Either way it is quite different to a man's behaviour, and the alarm bells are ringing.

The media treatment of women in the limelight whether they are business women or supermodels illustrates this point. The attention they receive is seldom without its degree of either overt or implied criticism. The supermodels and modern icons are invited to put themselves on display. It is after all good for sales. The favourite sport is then to put them under a magnifying glass and look for the flaws, faults in their lifestyle or clothes sense, proof that what they have achieved can't last, or is damaging to those they are supposed to care for.

It has always been much more difficult for a woman to have her head above the parapet than for a man. They immediately become more exposed, more vulnerable, all of which would appear to bear out Warren Lamb's claim that their combination of Growing Shape and Convex Shaping makes them more open to attack. Men on the other hand who protect themselves as they Grow have it much easier. It has always been OK for men to be out front, the leaders of every walk of life, and it is with astonishment and shock that we learn they have committed an 'inappropriate act' in a 'moment of weakness'. It is unusual for a man to so damage his career that there is no return. Failure in a woman is much more likely to be perceived as proof that she should not have been there in the first place, and there is seldom a reinstatement.

PUTTING ON THE PRESSURE

Differences are perhaps most noticeable between the sexes when each is being assertive. The use of Increasing Pressure is associated with stressing an argument, exerting authority or perhaps simply closing a lid on a rather full suitcase. When a woman uses Increasing Pressure she naturally combines it with Free Flow. There is inevitably some dissipation of the strength of the action, it appears to go into the air, become abandoned. The authority in the action is less powerful, as a means of argument less persuasive, and the suitcase would still not be shut.

A woman therefore has to find other ways of achieving her ends. She can persuade, for example by combining Binding Flow of Effort with Indirecting Effort, by talking all round the subject and gradually making her point. Positively performed this will be good, constructive and persuasive argument, at its worst it will be wheedling. An alternative is to exert authority by the Shaping of her movement – by Growing and Rising –giving an air of superiority and aloofness. This can be a highly effective way of controlling people without raising a finger. How many people's mothers "never laid a finger on them" and yet "ruled with a rod of iron"? As for closing the suitcase, again where Effort fails, Shape can help and the natural thing to do is to sit on the lid [Shrinking and Descending].

For a man to exercise strength is easier, patterned as it is with Binding Flow of Effort. The strength is contained, more controlled, more amenable to being directed, and the effect upon his audience will be significantly different. Picture again a [male] political speaker or an executive at a business meeting making a fist to hit the lectern or table as an expression of emphasis. He will be saying something like, "I insist that …". His Binding Flow of Effort will be accompanied with Contending Effort. The audience easily gets the message that he believes what he is saying, intends to do something about it, and he probably conveys authority, persuasiveness and command.

When women politicians emulate this male behaviour they give quite a different impression because it is unnatural for them to make all these combinations. By combining Increasing Pressure with Freeing Flow of Effort the action has an abandoned appearance instead of control. To combine it with Binding Flow of Effort would be performed as a gesture and very quickly would be perceived as such. It would lack sincerity and might even look comical. Supposing it is a question of getting a person to complete something on time or according to a definite programme. A woman giving instructions runs the risk of being bossy if her authority is not tempered with some humour or caring affection. Betty Boothroyd is the only woman to have held the position of Speaker of the British Parliament and kept order there most successfully, seeming to find just the right formula in dealing with a predominantly male House of Commons. On retirement they described her very fondly as combining her impressive political skills with the demeanour of a headmistress or nanny. Would a man in such an eminent and demanding position appreciate being called 'avuncular'?

It may appear from this that men are more effective at strong movements and forceful arguments than women, but this is only where there is a distinct association with control and tension, with keeping things in check. If the mood of the

Emphasising a point the female way. Freeing Flow of Effort
+ Contending Effort (Increasing Pressure)

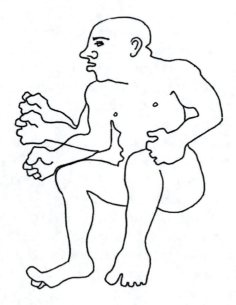

Emphasising a point the male way. Binding Flow of Effort
+ Contending Effort (Increasing Pressure)

speech is essentially to associate the "I insist ..." with aspirations for a freer, happier, or essentially altruistic objective, then women are extremely effective. There have been plenty of inspirational women to bear that out.

Assertion of strength comes into every aspect of life. Functionally it can be hammering a nail or holding a rebellious child; expressively it can be crying "Stop" to someone in danger. The experience of exerting strength however is very different for a woman, than for a man. For a woman asserting strength becomes associated with freedom, laissez-faire, swinging, letting go. Perhaps her psychology is preconditioned, simply by being a woman, that strength means freedom. Female expression of strength can seem to a man to be wild, emotional, subjective or even devious. Is this why men find 'strong' women so alarming? Do they feel they are out of control, might ride roughshod over them and simply disdain their male authority?

Women find it uncomfortable to be both strong and controlled. A nice result is that confronted with very Bound and Directed behaviour either their own or that of someone else, they will often dissolve into giggles. In a friendly women's tennis match if the players find themselves all at the net in a long volleying rally it will often break down in shrieks of laughter. It is as if they are not willing to tolerate the pressure except [gesturally] for a short time. Men on the other hand find volleying a natural even preferable way to play. If a man buys into strength it is not usually associated with a sense of humour, but much more with their need for discipline, control and constraint, all of which they are thoroughly comfortable with. The male expression of strength often seems to a woman to be forced, arbitrary and tense to the point of being inappropriate. Since it contains no humour, to laugh at it for being "over the top" will probably provoke the man to anger.

CARING AND SHARING

The combination of Freeing Flow of Effort with Contending Effort natural to women is useful for teachers or group leaders to use to bring a group of people together. "Hey guys, let's look at this interesting thing!" It can be a useful way of controlling a potentially unruly class of schoolchildren if carried off successfully. This same skill operates among a group of women quite naturally, enabling them to synchronise; they will both be Free and focussed. It is the ideal formula for a heart-to-heart, such as women are good at, completely relaxed but eager for detail! All-women meetings can be extremely successful for the same reason. They can deal efficiently with the business without the need for any of the protocol or ceremony necessary to their male counterparts.

When a woman tries to chat to a man in the same way she will be less successful. As he copies her in becoming relaxed he will also become unfocussed. "What was that you said, dear?" In this relaxed, Free mood he looks as if he finds it hard to care, and she feels he is not interested. The moment he changes to giving Attention, however, he combines this with Binding Flow of Effort, and the relaxed atmosphere is lost. She will say, "It isn't that important, why are you suddenly attacking me?"

Many attempts have been made to identify the differences between men and women in the way they communicate with each other, or fail to do so. Men do not easily express their feelings to a woman, and women feel men avoid talking things over. Women on the other hand want to discuss their feelings and fall more easily into communication on intimate subjects with other women.

The concept of Sharing initiative as distinct from keeping initiative Private has been discussed as an important concept in Action Profiling® and executive team-building [Chapter Five]. It is equally important in the realms of male/female interaction. By Sharing initiative here we mean a situation in which one person needs to draw the attention of another to a specific problem, to elicit that person's co-operation in deciding what should be done, and to jointly commit themselves to a plan of action.

If a person wants thoroughly to share the initiative of what he or she is giving attention to, to work as a team with someone, he or she ideally should exercise the affinities, as outlined earlier, between Shape and Effort. They have, for example, to combine Directing/Enclosing or Indirecting/Spreading. Assuming it is a woman who chooses to employ Directing/Enclosing, she is likely to also combine this with Freeing Flow of Effort and/or Shrinking [again use the chart to follow these combinations]. Her attitude will be that of someone eagerly getting down to something. She will come across as particularly keen to focus the other person on a specific point. "Let's sit down at the table and sort this out over a cup of tea!"

If that person is a man who wants to give his attention, he will do so by combining his Directing with Binding Flow of Effort and Enclosing with Growing. Suppose they are studying a map or chart laid out on the table.

He will think, "She seems to want my attention, but is very relaxed and easy about it and why is she withdrawing into her own world if she wants me to take an interest in this map?"

Meanwhile she sees him as Growing his kinesphere, and in danger of dominating her. This is not the cosy situation she anticipated. There is a potential for conflict immediately. She is asking for communication but withdrawing, and she is making the initiative but to him seems casual about it. In her perception he is threatening to swamp her, refusing to enter her world, become involved in the project with her. She also wonders why he is becoming so wound up about something they could sort out amicably. It would be equally difficult if the man took the initiative in inviting communication. She might feel too threatened and pressurised to be able properly to give the matter consideration.

One way to avoid the pressure would be for the man to counter the woman's Directing/Enclosing with his Indirecting/Spreading. They would then synchronise on Freeing Flow of Effort and Shrinking, but then another contradiction would arise. He leans back in a relaxed friendly way and she interprets this as a lack of interest, while he erroneously thinks his relaxed approach will give her an easy-going, ready to cooperate message.

"Come on, look at this map properly," she says.

"OK, OK," he says and hunches over it [Binding Flow of Effort and Directing Effort] so that she can't look at it at all. "Why can't we just look at it together?" she asks. And well she might. It is obviously a minefield, but a minefield that we all have ways of crossing in the majority of our day-to-day business. Either there is a clearly defined hierarchy of command, and we just have to get on with it, or we have intellectual or social skills to help us out. But wherever there is a lack of convention to determine who does what the problem will be exacerbated. Repetitions of this sort of scenario could well make each side feel that if they need to talk something over or have another opinion, they might do better to talk to/ work with a member of their own sex. At the same time it has to be remembered that harmony is not always the best way of achieving results, and the very dynamism created by the male/female interaction is important to making the world go round.

MAKING DECISIONS

The potential for either discord or dynamism is there at each stage of the Decision Making Process.

Attention Stage

Spreading/Indirecting by either side: A man will combine it with Freeing Flow of Effort/Shrinking, a woman with Binding Flow of Effort/Growing. She says: "Why are you being so casual about something I feel is important and drawing away from me when I want your close attention?" He says: "You seem so anxious and overbearing I'm going to hold back to protect myself."

Enclosing/Directing: A man combines it with Binding Flow of Effort/Growing; a woman with Freeing Flow of Effort/Shrinking. She says: "It's not so important that you have to get aggressive with me." He says: "For heaven's sake come here and pay attention to what I'm saying."

Intention Stage

Descending/Increasing Pressure: A man will combine it with Binding Flow of Effort/Growing, the woman with Freeing Flow of Effort/Shrinking. She says: "You seem anxious about facing up to this issue – have you got something to hide? And puffing yourself up like that just makes me feel you are trying to dominate me." He says: "If you really mean what you're saying, why are you so unconcerned about it, and why aren't you prepared to be fully involved in sorting it out?"

Rising/Decreasing Pressure: A man will combine it with Freeing Flow of Effort/Shrinking, a woman with Binding Flow of Effort/Growing. She says: "We know this is important but you seem unwilling to show any concern." He says: "Here I am gently and in a relaxed manner trying to understand what you think so important and are so assertive about, but all you try to do is smother me."

Commitment Stage

This again has its own problems. Imagine the couple are making an important purchase in a busy department store with all the decisions and anxieties it involves.

Retreating/Accelerating: A man will use Binding Flow of Effort/Growing; the woman Freeing Flow of Effort/Shrinking. She says: "I know we have to get in line but there is no need for you to be so tense and make such a scene about it." He says: "Do stop backing away just when we need to be together. You don't seem to want to stick with me and might wander off into another department."

Advancing/Decelerating: A man will use Freeing Flow of Effort/Shrinking, a woman Binding Flow of Effort/Growing. She says: "This waiting makes me anxious, and yet you seem so nonchalant. Why don't you get a bit more lively and do something instead of shrinking back into your own little world?" He says: "There's no point getting all worked up and making a fuss like that. Just stop trying to mother me and drag me along like a child."

Most of us can recognise something of ourselves in these situations. A woman is tense when a man is relaxed; she takes a high profile when he cautiously bides his time or vice versa. On a good day they will be a dynamic partnership, on a bad day quite incompatible, each certain that the other has precisely the wrong attitude. Human relations can be so fragile, but most of the time the simplicity of the misunderstanding eludes us. If our understanding of the language of physical behaviour was as advanced as our knowledge of the spoken word we might all rub along rather better.

VIVE LA DIFFERENCE

Given the inherent differences in the way men and women quite literally behave, there is a strong case for this being taken on board when discussing their roles both at work and in society. It is rather naïve, surely, to think that, given the rather noticeable biological difference between the sexes and the different functions they perform in propagating the species, that the differences go no further than that, or that it is somehow something we can entirely control, perhaps ignore.

Unfortunately it is confused by the question of value. Women have been groomed to behave like a minority when in fact most of the time they have been in a numerical majority. It would be wrong to think that men alone have been the designers of that grooming. Women in charge of rearing girls can be more repressive than any man. But the attitude persists and is reflected in the consistently lower salaries paid to even the most senior women today.

Throughout history women have felt that to be liberated from subjugation, to rule anything from a boardroom to a nation, they had to emulate men. The Egyptian queen Hatshepsut as long ago as the 15th Century BC ruled her country for 21 years with unprecedented power, but to do so adopted the full paraphernalia of a Pharaoh, even including a false beard. "Power dressing" with large, masculine shoulder pads was fashionable in the 1980s as the career woman image. The changes in career and social opportunities for women in the lst two decades have not substantially altered this apparent need to assume a degree of male aggression.

Even though they can now share in opportunities, the changes in attitude by either side are not keeping pace. To add to the frustration and resentment, girls are expected to be equal achievers in school and college, but then to accept lower status the moment they qualify. Survey after survey dwells on the problem. Are working women properly paid, happy, satisfied, guilty? Should there be free nursery care, paid maternity/paternity leave? One survey claimed that 80% of wives would leave work if they could afford it. A survey of men at work might have come up with a similar result!

It has been assumed that the fight for women's rights if fought hard enough and long enough would result in equality, equality in status, pay and respect. This is patently not working. There is somewhere a missing link and it refuses to be forged by any amount of legislation or militancy. Perhaps it is because the wrong battle has been engaged in. Perhaps everyone is missing the point. A woman can never be "more like a man" – without, like Queen Hatshepsut, looking rather strange. And New Man, who was supposed to share equally in domestic responsibilities is a rare and floundering species. No act of will is going to make men and women the same.

To concentrate on what is similar – or should be – between the sexes is like going to the theatre and missing the point of the play, misunderstanding the plot. It is not the similarities but the differences which need to be examined, and these would seem to be more subtle and fascinating than we have ever understood. When they are taken on board perhaps real progress can be made.

In a number of areas because of their differing movement patterns, men will be more naturally talented than women, and in an equal number of areas women will outshine men. This is something to be appreciated not denied. There are also areas where they are equally talented, but they would find different routes to achieve the same end. In showing leadership, for example, a woman does better to be inspirational rather than assertive, whereas a man can be assertive about particular goals. To try to emulate each other in such behaviour is not a solution. It denies their natural talents.

Laban taught that individuality is of paramount importance, and for healthy living it must be preserved. Femininity and masculinity are part of those individual characteristics and we will all be the losers if we ignore that.

CHAPTER EIGHT

ALL THE WORLD'S A STAGE

Thee efficacy of Movement Pattern Analysis has been extensively tried and tested in the world of executive selection and team-building, where its few practitioners have successfully applied it for fifty years. In that time it has developed into a highly sophisticated instrument with its reliability proven in a rigorous and cost-conscious environment. Deborah du Nann Winter has argued that it is regrettable these techniques have not been researched and developed to serve a wider social purpose, and some possible areas where it could be either applied or misapplied are touched on here. At the same time there is an argument that perhaps the very fact that the validity of Movement Pattern Analysis has gone through its development in the commercial world may help it to be accepted seriously in areas of therapy, gender and social issues – in other words as a common denominator to all aspects of life.

MOVEMENT AND POLITICS

When he was arranging mass pageants in the 1920s Laban developed his theory of national rhythm. He claimed blacksmiths making horseshoes in different countries made them to different rhythms, and these rhythms reflected that of their national dance. Experiments carried out on behalf of Action Profiling® have shown that groups predominating in the Attention range of movement came up with entirely different suggestions for solving problems from groups predominating in the Intention or Commitment range. The solutions they all proposed were in line with the predominant movement characteristics of each group. How things are done therefore accords with the movement patterns of the people involved. In making a horseshoe the results are effectively the same, but in solving social or managerial problems, the outcome from one group to another, is quite different.

Once a movement has been done it cannot be undone; it can only be overtaken by the next movement. If all the people in a room or at a rally make the same type of movements, in response, say, to a speech or a type of music, it impacts upon the mood of the group as a whole, and dictates the atmosphere in the room. They will become happy or sad, enthusiastic or angry, aggressive or gentle, according to the nature of the speech or music. If the speaker or the music changes, so will the mood and behaviour of the group.

It is easy to see how powerful movement can be when exercised by large groups of people. An assembly of men, potentially the more aggressive, exercising Freeing Flow of Effort and Indulging Effort – as one imagines was the case with the Flower People in San Francisco in the 1960s – can be compared with a group of men exercising Binding Flow of Effort with Contending Effort as at a Hitler rally. It has long been known that the physical behaviour of large groups can be manipulated and used for social and political purposes but even without any control, national characteristics in movement exist and smaller groups assume an identity according to the predominant characteristics in them. These characteristics go much deeper than hand gestures or facial expressions and skilled political leaders have always known how to whip up support into a fervour.

This is often done by inventing a behaviour which binds their followers together with gestures, styles of walking and the like. National characteristics, if Kestenberg is to be believed, must also be formed to a large degree in the crib by the traditions of caring for babies and, if this is the case, could future generations be manipulated into compliance by these subtle means, without the need for overt indoctrination?

In a three week summer school in the 1980s Warren Lamb demonstrated how easily this can be done by creating a Cult of the Diagonal Scale. Each morning his 20 or so students practiced the diagonal scale, and to drive home the importance of it in movement he developed this into an elaborate game. They not only practiced the scale, but also composed songs and created chants and dances to celebrate it. For three weeks the Diagonal Scale was celebrated in every possible way. By the end of the course a veritable religion had been built around the diagonal and the students had to remind themselves that it had all started as a game.

MOVEMENT ANALYSIS AND THERAPY

The work done by Warren Lamb with Kestenberg and Bartenieff was inevitably to some extent a two-way process. The period in the fifties and early sixties was a formative time for Warren Lamb, and after Laban's death his increased communication with many of Laban's disciples was significant to his own development. It was not entirely coincidental that it was at this time that he formed his theory of the Posture-Gesture Merger as the blueprint of individual movement.

While he had a large impact on their thinking, he also drew from them, and during this period a significant amount of his work was in movement as a therapy.

132

In fact the only part of his work ever to receive public funding was with disturbed and mentally ill patients. This particular area has been explored much less in Britain than in the United States. Although training centres in for example, dance therapy, do exist in Britain the emphasis tends to be on work with children with learning difficulties. This limited application is a pity since, as a non-intrusive method of helping people to – literally – a more balanced life, it seems movement therapy could be so valuable.

This point was made by Warren Lamb after a demonstration given to a group of Jungian psychiatrists in 1952. The conference was at Withy Meade in Devon and the group were carrying out pioneering work on art and dance therapy. Warren Lamb, working in conjunction with his first wife, Joan Carrington, summed up what they had done:

"You will have noticed that all this has taken place without any reference to the patient's emotions or dreams and without extracting any personal details whatsoever. In fact we deliberately avoid if possible any discussion of private life and would not be so presumptuous as to advise our clients on the conduct of their affairs ... contrary to some forms of psycho-analysis, we accept solely the situation of the present and are not interested in causes."

It was consistent with Jung's theories to encourage people to dance or to act out their stresses in movement, or to align with the ritualistic practices of some other society. Lamb questioned whether what the psychiatric patients did was always good for them, or if it was possibly the reverse in many cases. He argued that it was necessary to thoroughly understand a patient's individual movement pattern before getting them to move in a particular way. Not to do so would be potentially dangerous for the patient.

It had always been his belief that once the ratio between each stage of movement is formed it is dangerous to alter it. For example if the Attention Stage was less well developed than the other two stages, perhaps like this:

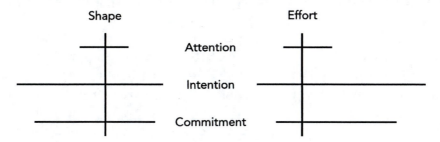

Fig. 18. Effort and shape graph for someone low in Attention range of movement

– it would be dangerous then to try to develop that range without also extending the other two in order to maintain the balance. The argument appealed to several psychiatrists and Lamb found himself for a while giving movement therapy to groups of their patients. It was not without its difficulties. He had to be careful to give individual attention and make sure that group fervour did not overtake them.

In one group there was a couple, Mr and Mrs B. who went to a number of classes and gave the appearance of enjoying them immensely. Suddenly they stopped attending. After a time Warren Lamb asked their psychiatrist if she had an explanation. "Yes," she said, "I worked with Mr and Mrs B. for several years on their failure to conceive a child and they eventually accepted that having a family was not for them. But after attending a number of your classes Mrs B. told me she began to feel that she might be able to conceive a child after all, and I had to tell her to stop attending the classes."

Something like 100 courses of 10 sessions were also given to individuals, among them an art critic, a concert pianist and business executives. After finding in which way the individuals could adjust their movement pattern to improve their well-being or solve some particular problem, Warren Lamb would often devise a simple exercise which could be built into their daily behaviour. This would serve to remind them of the work they had done in their session with him and would help to make the new movement part of their established behaviour. The aim was always to release potential in the individual, potential which had been blocked by some experience in earlier life. Most significantly the problem could be addressed without the necessity of having to recall that experience. The concert pianist was so impressed by the help he received from movement analysis he suggested to Warren Lamb that they should document the experience. The resulting manuscript languished unpublished until it was revived two years ago. In its conclusion the authors, Warren Lamb and Ronald Meachen, touched on the point where performers of all kinds can benefit from an understanding of their own movement pattern:

"This gives rise to a new concept of technique, which may now be defined as the performer's ability to obtain from the instrument any desired musical effect by a means which accords with his own range of effort. Any attempt to exceed this range will result in a sensation of discomfort, either physiological or psychological."

The research grant Lamb received was for work with six mental patients at St Bernard's Hospital in London. He found it essential to give each a personal movement routine to help their problems. A common feature of movement in a mentally ill person would, for example, be a 'locking' of movement in one extreme or another of a range of movement. The patient might be at the extreme end of movement in that range, or perhaps hardly began to move in that range at all. Some people will swing from one extreme to another, others will leave an extreme position briefly only to return to it again. Being locked in this sense can indicate despair, grief, or being just plain lost, and in movement can be described and treated without being analysed or interpreted. The danger is that in inexperienced hands exactly the wrong range of movement might be used. Thinking back to the different aspects of Shape, Effort and Flow, it can be appreciated that in skilled hands it is possible to isolate the area of movement which needs to be developed to restore balance to a person's behaviour. To work on the wrong area of movement would only lead to increasing the anxiety of the patient.

The counselling element has never been far removed from Lamb's work. In making assessments for management appointments or in career guidance he was always concerned to advise people on their particular aptitudes and where their shortcomings might prove a problem. If they were not suitable for the position under consideration, he would advise them on how else they might use their talents. True to Laban's philosophy, an interview for a position should not be regarded as a test to be passed but an exploration of possibilities given the nature of the individual. Similarly in movement as a therapy the concern was always to work towards the best that was available for that individual and not towards a fixed ideal.

RITUALISED BEHAVIOUR

Another area briefly explored by Warren Lamb and one which would benefit from further research, is the relationship between Integrated Movement, or the Posture-Gesture Merger, and addictive or ritualised behaviour. In a study he made of people smoking, he found that addictive smokers used their Posture Gesture Merger at every stage of the business of dealing with their cigarette or pipe. This could be carried through the process of, for example, lighting the cigarette, tapping off the ash, cleaning the pipe, dealing with the ashtray, even actually sucking on the pipe or cigarette. The whole series of operations were so smooth and obviously carefully enjoyed with all their favourite movements as to be positively ritualistic. In smokers who were able to take or leave the habit and were intermittent smokers, PGM played only a minor part.

Warren Lamb – an icosahedron is in the background

This would suggest that it is much more difficult to stop smoking when it is a deeply integrated part of a person's behaviour pattern. It is then an addiction. The statement is almost a truism, but it serves the purpose of indicating what may be an easier and safer way of breaking an addiction than hypnosis. If smoking is part of one's favourite movement pattern it is actually a prop allowing the movement sequence to take place. Take away the prop and the person is disorientated. He cites the case of a woman who would make a long diagonal movement to drop ash into an ashtray, even to the extent of actually pushing the ashtray a little away from her to give the movement more Sagittal stress and make it more to her liking. Then there are the smokers who will throw an arm across the back of a chair, ostensibly to avoid bothering their companions with their smoke, when they are in fact bothering the people on the next table instead. Do they really need to make such a big movement to get the same result? The ritual gives them the excuse for doing what they like best.

The non-addicted smoker will often be characterised by the awkwardness of their movements, simply because it is not part of their integrated behaviour. They seem to make much more smoke and to consistently puff it into their companion's faces. They forgetfully drop their ash on the floor and the furniture, fastidiously fiddle with the ashtray, and although they may smoke less, their smoking can be much more evident than that of an addict. Of course if they keep trying they might eventually get there. It is the route of all addictions. But some people are simply not addictive types and as long as they remain a non-addicted smoker there is no gap to fill in their behaviour pattern when they decide to abandon nicotine. For the addict it will be that much more difficult unless something replaces the behavioural ritual. Nicotine patches and sucking mints will only partially fill the bill. This is another area therefore where movement analysis could perhaps make a positive contribution by building a replacement movement pattern for the addict.

In other cases a ritual can actually be developed to help a person cope with a problem. Warren Lamb cites as an illustration the case of a stammerer he treated. A particular problem the patient had every day was asking for his bus fare. He found it intensely difficult to tell the bus-conductor where he was going and of course the more he dreaded it the worse it became. The words would not come out on cue. Warren Lamb devised for the sufferer a movement ritual which he could go into as the conductor approached. To any onlooker it would simply look as if he was rummaging in his pockets for money, but it would start with a fairly complicated postural adjustment and move into another as he stretched into a diagonal and put his hand into his pocket, speaking the necessary words as the hand came up. The patient found the little ritual could be adapted for many occasions.

SOCIAL CONSIDERATIONS OF MOVEMENT AND GENDER

The Gender War was at pains to prove there was no difference between men and women, and this in itself became a fashion game, certain to confuse more than it solved. First there were unisex hair salons and unisex clothes, then there were unisex jobs and anti-discrimination laws.

To understand the intrinsic differences between men and women in movement we have first to clear our minds of the "body language" tricks devised to exploit masculinity and femininity. Advertising, pop culture and the media generally have invented a whole language of pseudo gestures, a shorthand to spell out the ideal man or woman you will become if you buy such-and-such a product. It is good business and can be good fun when it is not too exploitative of human weakness. Fashion is related to the mores of the time, and also moulds the style of movement current at any particular time. But such movements are superficial and simply mask the individuality of behaviour or the gender differences in movement.

True expression of male and female behaviour needs no props or poses. Watch children of two years old playing. A group of boys will play much more aggressively and physically than a group of girls. They do not need to be dressed in special clothes to look masculine or feminine. If a boy wants to keep a toy for himself he will probably gather it in [Concave Shaping] while Growing his kinesphere – grasp it with one arm and be ready to punch with the other. A girl wanting to keep her toy will gather it to her [Concave Shaping] but with a Shrinking of her kinesphere. Like her mother holding a baby, she seems to say "My toy and I have chosen this space – don't invade!" This typical male/female behaviour is seen a lot in small children. It does not mean Growing Shape Flow is exclusive to boys and Shrinking Shape Flow to girls. Girls would Grow, for example, when openly offering their toy to someone, and they would combine it with Convex Shaping. If a boy were similarly moved to be generous, he would probably combine it with Shrinking. Neither sex is being more protective or more generous – simply different at being both.

Aggressiveness is perhaps the favourite way of comparing girls and boys. Most findings show that boys are physically more aggressive than girls, and that their aggression is tolerated more than it would be in girls. Schoolboys call out more in class, they are happier to risk getting the answer wrong than the relatively cautious girls. Girls make up for it by being more verbally aggressive when the chance arises.

The advantages of educating children in movement to guard against particular physical problems such as RSI was touched on in an earlier chapter. Every child in a prosperous country faces a future potentially dominated by the sedentary use of technology both in leisure and in work. There is an argument for the national curriculum to include training in understanding how to protect one's physique against this and every other type of common injury. It could save millions in hours lost from work and in health bills. What's more it would be fun.

But an understanding of good movement goes much further towards improving the quality of life. Learning one's own movement pattern is the simplest start to understanding oneself. No amount of astrology or psychology will give such practical information. A simple understanding of one's physical behaviour produces practical information and enables a greater empathy with others. It helps the individual to develop coping mechanisms for difficult situations. Short people, for example, very often have ways of making themselves look bigger and assertive in a crowd. They can "puff themselves up" and almost dance from one foot to the other while addressing a group to occupy a bigger space, and it can be very effective in making them appear bigger. Just as a physically handicapped person can learn ways of compensating for his or her disability, so can everyone be helped to deal with their social and personal problems and guided towards a more fulfilling life.

Laban is still alive and well in physical education, especially in secondary education where expressive dance is a popular part of the PE curriculum. The mass dancing in clubs and discos today would probably thrill him. It would seem that other aspects of movement education could be equally as enjoyable and worthwhile. It would be much more today than women doing 'light' movements and men 'strong' movements. Laban was always in the vanguard of thought in his day, and he would have made no exception of modern problems such as RSI, dysfunctional social behaviour and the Gender War.

PERSONAL RELATIONSHIPS

An understanding of the impact of our physical behaviour on others is a practical start to knowing how to improve one's relationships. We usually know when we have said something to upset other people, but why are they sometimes hostile when we have said nothing at all? In a structured society where behaviour is mannered and the rules are clear the process of for example making a new acquaintance simply follows a set of rules. Restrictive though this is, it is probably easier to avoid the painful misunderstandings of today's fluid relationships. Today when boy meets girl and they go on their first date they may each have only a hazy idea of what the other regards as appropriate behaviour. They will have to watch each other for signals of approval or disapproval to know the other's intentions.

Supposing the girl is relaxed and confident [Freeing Flow of Effort + Contending Effort], the boy will feel his new girlfriend is confident in company [good] and happy to meet his friends [good]. But he may feel she gives more attention to others than to him [bad]. If she is too Free, of course, she will embarrass him and get herself a 'bad name'. She may alternatively seem controlled and withdrawn [Binding Flow of Effort + Indulging Effort] and would probably show comparatively little interest in those around her. Both are potentially dangerous and many relationships will founder on these early rocks.

The girl, too, would need to feel confident about her new young man. Walking into a party he may be free and relaxed, sociably giving his attention to all and sundry [good], but if this goes too far she will feel she has no special place in his life [bad] and need not be there. At least for the boy there is no danger of his ebullience damaging his reputation. For him it just shows him to be a 'great guy' or 'one of the boys'. On the other hand his behaviour might be entirely focussed on one person – hopefully her – which may or may not be good depending on how she feels about him.

By the use of Effort Flow, a woman in a man's eyes is either a free being looking for something to give her attention to, and if it is him he will have her full attention; or she is a controlled being whose attention is given equally to everyone. A man in a woman's eyes is either a free being whose attention is all over the place and that will probably include other women; or he is a controlled being who signals precisely what he is interested in and it may well be her.

The different use of Flow of Shape means that a man seems to confidently Grow towards a social gathering whilst at the same time being careful not to lay himself open to criticism. He can alternatively take a back seat [Shrink] and watch the proceedings from the edge of the room before taking any action. A woman in a man's eyes can be freely open to the assembled group, either as a charming hostess, or at the other extreme as a terrible flirt. Alternatively she may be the original shrinking violet watching everyone nervously and appearing too shy or disinterested to speak.

This difference in behaviour extends to more general social problems. Binding Flow of Effort is a natural attribute to control and thus to problem solving. Since the sexes phrase it differently with Effort and Shape, their approaches to problem solving are different. When a man uses Binding Flow of Effort together with Contending Effort he encourages those around him to tighten up, to become more assertive. He may well do this for example in reaction to something offending his beliefs. He creates a tension, and with Directing Effort, this tension is aimed at a very specific point. He will, if he can, identify and deal with the specific cause of his concern. The matter will be closed.

When a woman creates the sense of tension by her Binding Flow of Effort she combines it with Indulging Effort, so that her Attention is not focussed on, say, one person, object or issue, but on a group of factors. If the man and woman are together in giving Attention to the same matter she may feel that the man is being arbitrary in his accusation by singling out one person or thing to blame. She may feel that the whole situation needs changing. When a neighbourhood is threatening, for example, a man's response is to pinpoint the culprit and take action; the woman's may be to take against the whole neighbourhood and move house.

Of course the need to use Binding Flow of Effort can occur in many situations other than those involving threat. It may be a way of exercising care. Binding Flow of Effort with Directing Effort, the male preference, seems appropriate to surgery, which may explain why that part of the medical profession attracts more men than women. Binding Flow of Effort with Indirecting Effort, the female preference, is more appropriate for care and watchfulness, qualities required in nursing. It may not be entirely social and cultural factors that have decided how many of each sex go into the different areas of the medical profession. Exceptions will always be found, and there are many more facets to such skilled work than this particular aspect of movement. There are also many successful women surgeons who have knowledge and skills to match any man. But where their work requires Binding Flow of Effort with Directing Effort it would be performed as a series of gestures, and would be difficult to sustain for long. Some element of integration into a whole body movement would eventually be necessary.

Research carried out by Du Nann Winter [Chpt 5] on the subject of choice of profession and aptitude is interesting in this context. Here a definite relationship was found between aptitude according to Movement Analysis and the choice of career. If these findings are reliable, it follows that given particular movement patterns defining the sexes, there would also be a difference in the type of work they feel more comfortable with, and would for the most part choose. This encourages the thought that perhaps we are expecting too much from ourselves in expecting all jobs to be unisex! This is not to suggest that women should not be, say, long-distance lorry drivers or soldiers. It is simply to say that we should not lose sleep over them being in the minority in any job except where there is positive discrimination. Many jobs which have traditionally been done by the opposite sex can certainly be done by both, but in many cases trying too hard to emulate the opposite sex will result in some form of stress.

If there was ever a misconception that one sex is 'free' and the other controlled in behaviour, hopefully the record has been put straight. Men and women can both be predominantly free or controlled, but use them differently and in doing so will create different impressions. To say someone has Freeing Flow of Effort means that they have a tendency towards that end of the polarity between Bound and Free, but they will have some element of 'control' as well. The Flow of their movement must reverse at some time. Only skilled observation can assess where on the scale the movement occurs between the polarities of rigid and abandoned although, if we think about it, we will intuitively know the answer for those closest to us fairly well. The differences become of greatest importance when it affects the perception in another person of what we are about. Like young people on their first date, adults can equally get upset quite irrationally by their perception of each other's attitudes.

PUNISHMENT AND REHABILITATION

These differences in the physical behaviour of the sexes are relevant when dealing with social policies. If men and women have different movement patterning and react differently to situations, it follows that to be efficient, treatment of men and women with similar problems should also be different.

Take for example the treatment of young people who are presented for rehabilitation after developing a drug problem and living rough. The behaviour of such people is probably excessively towards the Freeing Flow of Effort polarity; it needs to have some tension built into it to move them towards the Bound end of the spectrum. They need to be given control, resistance and discipline. Treatment for women in such cases, according to Warren Lamb, needs to be built on a relaxed system with a lot of sleep, pleasurable activities, having things done for them. The aim would be to reverse the tendency to Freeing Flow of Effort and Contending Effort [fighting everything] and move their behaviour towards the opposite polarities of Binding Flow of Effort with Indulging Effort. They need a regime, but it should be one with gentleness and caring built into it.

For men the opposite has to apply. A man in such a situation would need to be moved away from Freeing Flow of Effort and Indulging Effort [letting it all hang out] to Binding Flow of Effort and Contending Effort. The regime in this case should be strict with a disciplined timetable, goals to be met, rules to be obeyed. Perhaps those old-fashioned boys' schools and RSMs sometimes had the right idea if not always the right methods!

Men and women also respond differently to dangerous situations. If a woman finds herself vulnerable in a social situation she can help herself by relating to it with a Shrinking movement. She will then identify herself with a restricted field and find that easier to cope with. She will either protect herself or find protection. If a man finds he is vulnerable in some way he needs to Grow, to identify himself with the larger picture. There is perhaps a case for saying women prefer to Shrink from danger and men to Grow towards it, but this in no way implies that women are less brave than men, or that men are more foolhardy than women. Every situation has to be judged on its own merits. The relative preferences are important however, in choosing ways of coping with difficult circumstances.

Living in a poor urban area where there is a threat of violence would illustrate these differences. Where she is afraid of being attacked a woman will instinctively shrink, gather in and close everything around her. Locking doors and windows will be a priority. When she goes out she will carefully avoid eye contact with people she doesn't trust, try to be anonymous or invisible. A man may also shrink away in self-defence, but in doing so he will be sure to face his opposition and keep them under surveillance. He is more likely to get into confrontation than a woman. A man is also more likely to seek protection by joining one side or the other where there is a gang culture.

Supposing, however, although it is a bad neighbourhood, a woman does not herself feel personally threatened. She may, as women in Northern Ireland have for example, feel that she wants to do something to improve the community. She will do this by Growing towards the community, demonstrating an openness, a willingness to talk publicly, to communicate, to listen. People will feel she is willing to do anything to help. A man feeling the same urge to Grow towards the community would do so with a more closed attitude. He would offer his help in a more selective way, choosing the people to work with to support his leadership. He would be altogether more carefully political.

MOVEMENT AS A COMMON DENOMINATOR

As long as people are alive they are moving whatever they are doing, from writing a classical novel to washing the dishes, from cleaning the windows on a skyscraper to digging the garden. Whatever they are doing they are moving, and in a way quite individual to them. Business managers may be more interested in profitability and sales figures, doctors in test results, but they both know that they have also intuitively gained essential information about the people they are dealing with by an instinctive reading of their physical behaviour. The popular description for what people do in this sense is to "read their Body Language". Sports commentators regularly report on the change in a competitor's Body Language between the time when they are winning to the moment they are facing defeat. Such observations are totally valid and convey their point clearly. We are all conscious of a change in deportment between elation and dejection, joy and despair, interest and boredom, energy and exhaustion.

As must be clear however, Movement Analysis sees beyond this and is a more subtle tool for reading what is permanent in a person's movement pattern. It is not concerned with temporary attitudes of sadness or lethargy, but will detect the potential in the person whatever they are feeling at any given moment. A study of Body Language can be useful but it is concerned with the here and now interpretation of attitudes, and attitudes are temporary and worse, can be contrived for whatever occasion. Movement Analysis is never concerned with positions or attitudes, but only with movement, and the basic pattern of a person's movement will emerge for the skilled observer no matter how hard the individual tries to contrive it, or in whatever context the observations are made.

Movement is therefore a common denominator of life. Laban believed movement should have equal importance in our working life, social life or spiritual life. In all of these we have to move and in doing so we express our individuality and to do so should be a joy. Movement identifies with all activity whether the activity is serious, trivial, intellectual or physical. Understanding movement therefore has a contribution to make in almost every area of social life – education, health, rehabilitation of all kinds, quite apart from its demonstrated use in business management.

One aspect of movement study – that favoured by the Alexander Technique – recognises that to understand how we are moving will improve 'personal efficiency'. With this approach we are not so likely to injure our backs from lifting heavy weights, leaning over the kitchen sink, or bending over a basin brushing our teeth. Many injuries are caused by simple everyday tasks carried out with movement which strains the body. These aspects of movement were partly Laban's concern in his early work at Dartington, at Tyresoles and at Mars, and Laban and Lamb met with Alexander on more than one occasion. But, as the mounting scale of case settlements for RSI proves, the lessons have never been seriously taken on board by either industrialists or educationalists.

Laban's overwhelming concern was with the spiritual joy of movement, not with the mere mechanical efficiency of it. His view of movement as a common denominator which should bring grace to every aspect of life has been embedded in Warren Lamb's work from the beginning.

Movement is part of every human activity. Analysis of it is worthwhile because a language of terms and a system of notation exist which can be used to record the phrases, rhythms, harmonies, and shapes of personal movement. To understand what is being seen in order to make a proper use of that information requires disciplined observation and notation. If such a record is obtained before interpretation is attempted, it can be put alongside other information and data relevant to that person's situation.

"Movement can be looked upon as a sixth sense, the Kinaesthetic Sense," says Warren Lamb. "The question arises, in what respect is the Kinaesthetic Sense more of a common denominator than the other five? It is difficult to imagine how the study of sound, sight, touch, smell and taste can be usefully related to anything like the range of activity which is the case with movement."

APPENDIX I

Paper by Warren Lamb presented to the conference "Views of Rudolf Laban from the 21st Century". School of Performing Arts, University of Surrey, 6th May 2000.

There is a theory that we are motivated to make decisions in a uniquely individual way according to how we move and Rudolf Laban did the groundwork for it. Assuming there is evidence to support it then why not apply Laban's discoveries to himself. In other words, if we can understand the relevant features of his own individual way of moving it may throw some new light on aspects of his personality and what motivated him to behave the way he did.

Surprisingly, little has been attempted, even by those who spent time with him, to describe how he moved. Most Laban students, particularly women, felt that he understood the essence of their being by means of perception of their movement. There was acceptance then that each person does have her or his own distinctively individual pattern of movement. My intention is to turn the tables, as it were, and see what clues we can get from reconstruction of Laban's own movement.

What Laban did by creative talent and charisma I have tried to emulate by means of discipline and hard work. Notation or film of Laban, from which to make a disciplined analysis, is not available. I do have diary notes, however, from the considerable amount of time I spent travelling to lectures, teaching engagements, movement observation sessions within industry, and from my experience of working closely with him on the methods which eventually became known as Action Profiling and now Movement Pattern Analysis.

From these diary notes I have had the temerity to try and reconstruct how Laban moved and, from the data thus collected, make an analysis and match it against the decision-making model. The result is a measure of Laban's preferred way of going through a decision-making process. There is, of course, a lot of conjecture involved and I would not attempt to do this with anyone else. It may have helped towards getting some degree of objectivity that I never hero worshipped Laban although I found him fascinating and spoke of him as a genius. Like everyone else, he could be fallible, and I never respected his propensity for acting like a guru.

Practitioners of Movement Pattern Analysis insist that observed movement data is essential for analysis so I am breaking the rules. The framework of terms derived from movement theory can be used, and regrettably often is, without reference to movement data and the result is then something quite different from an MPA and gives a different type of information.

Many of you will be familiar with this framework and the decision-making model. However, perhaps I should take a few minutes to recapitulate it. Its use based on movement data provides information on a person's uniquely preferred way of going through a decision-making process. We may not be able to follow our preference because of circumstances but it is always there. If too much of our action is contrary to this pattern of preference we suffer some form of stress. Accordingly, we are usually motivated to act from within our preferred pattern of movement – call it 'comfort zone' if you like – and this influences, for example, how we interpret responsibility, the nature of our personal relationships, and whether or not we achieve a sense of satisfaction in our work and play activities.

The model derives from Laban's alignment of Space effort with the first stage of ATTENTION, Weight with INTENTION, and Time with the actual DECISION to go through a point of no return. Laban did not himself see it as a sequence of stages or a process, however. Also he confined his work with me on movement observation and assessment to Effort. Shortly before he died I asked him if there was any reason why I should not incorporate observation of how the people I was observing Shaped their movement and after a surprised reaction he agreed it would be good to do so. My attempt to do this eventually led to this Framework of six initiatives [Fig. 19]. Please accept this very brief explanation of terms as an outline introduction necessary for understanding Laban's decision-making preferences.

Here is my attempt [Fig. 20] at an estimate of Rudolf Laban's Profile using reconstructed movement data against the model. Percentages are used as a means of showing relative preference and it is important to consider the pattern as a whole.

When I do a Movement Pattern Analysis I am often surprised that the Profile is different from my non-movement based impressions and that applies in this case.

Laban has a reputation as a researcher but, according to this Profile, he prefers to take initiative at the Commitment to action stage [41%] which suggests that his proclivity for getting action, while paramount, derives from a lot of proactive giving of Attention. He transfers easily from one to the other without much initiative to establish what his Intention is [10%]. There is not much emphasis on all that pertains to Intention: "What do I want, believe, consider right or wrong? What do I have to overcome to get the action I am interested in? What are my needs, convictions, and what must I do to adjust to the realities of the situation?" These are questions which Laban would tend not to ask – he was not motivated to take these sorts of Intention initiatives.

On the Perspective side Exploring and Anticipating are both high in order of preference. To the extent that each of these initiatives can be summarised in one word it can be said that the outcome of Exploring is ideas and the outcome of Anticipating vision – at least potentially. Laban's universally recognised creativity would derive mostly from a combination of the two with the likelihood that his vision ran ahead of his ideas. He must have felt encouraged to translate his fertile ideas into a visionary commitment [Anticipating is at the Commitment end of the decision-making process] because he was not motivated very much to Evaluate. It did not matter whether or not his ideas were realistic so long as he could project them. Another way of interpreting this point is that he wanted to take up a forward position with regard to his ideas from which he would be reluctant to go backward in the decision-making process for re-appraisal. It was more attractive to Laban to come up with still more ideas! Together with high Timing, which can be summarised as opportunism and a tendency to dictate the pace, Laban sought to practice what I might presume to call a runaway creativity, ignoring or circumnavigating any obstacles rather than pausing to combat them.

Absence of much motivation to Evaluate will have discouraged Laban from making black/white judgements; shades of grey would be preferred. He does have some Evaluating as a low order of preference so he would not be all that evasive. Together with low Determining, however, he would tend to put a smokescreen around challenges if he could, and mysticism would attract him as providing an appropriate context. It suited him to claim, as he repeatedly did, that life is a constant state of flux.

The combination of high Timing with high Anticipating in the pattern of his Profile has a form of harmony i.e. the Effort [Assertion] and Shape [Perspective] balance each other and this would have encouraged Laban to plunge into organising activity. He is motivated to take risks towards a vision of where he is going without first establishing a clarity of purpose which can only come from Intention initiatives.

There is a similar form of harmony between his Investigating and Exploring [with the Exploring component much the more evident] and there will be a link between these two forms of harmony i.e. between Timing and Anticipating on the one hand and Investigating and Exploring on the other hand. He would want to preserve this 'feel good' harmony, another reason for self promoting his runaway, visionary, opportunist, organisatory commitment to action and avoid the, for him, discordant initiative of taking a stand on some clearly evaluated issue.

It is a feature of our pattern of movement that we want to take a lead in pro-actively taking the predominant initiatives. Laban probably preferred to take the lead in Exploring, Anticipating and Timing, and let others take the lead in Determining, Evaluating and to some extent Investigating. He would probably reject anyone else's attempt to Explore independently of him, for example, but be more likely to accept their initiative to Investigate. He would also often want to reject others who were taking an independent lead in Timing and Anticipating preferring to follow his own programme and vision. Having taken these leads, however, his motivation to share his initiatives with others [see below] would make him open to support.

There is always a positive and a negative potential to all six initiatives. High Determining can be associated with pressurising and high Evaluating with black/white over-simplification, neither of which would appeal to Laban.

Of course, many other factors, including culture, conditioning, and genes, will have influenced his behaviour. On the basis of this Profile, however, I suggest that he would be oppressed by some sets of circumstances which others would deal with more as a challenge. He was frequently ill. I am not suggesting that all people who are frequently ill have the same Profile as this. What I do suggest is that Laban was not a 'head on' fighter and it may have suited him to retreat when he felt he could not maintain his creative progressiveness.

There is also a form of affinity between the Investigating and Exploring, and the Timing and Anticipating, which can be interpreted according to MPA theory that he was motivated to share these initiatives. Such a readiness to share ideas and vision would attract people to him and his runaway organisatory initiative would sweep people along with him. He could create an environment which was both highly communicative and operational. I am sure that this does not fully explain his charisma or remarkable attractiveness to women; it may be part of it, however. He certainly invited people to him who wanted to give him support, and this is consistent with high sharing and little need for privacy.

Those same people might also experience the occasional outbursts of criticism and condemnation which Laban was addicted to, which he himself acknowledged, and which the Profile suggests were an aspect of not being able to cope with frustrations of programming. This could possibly be associated with acts of ruthlessness.

FRAMEWORK OF MANAGEMENT INITIATIVE
THE MOTIVATION TO ACT

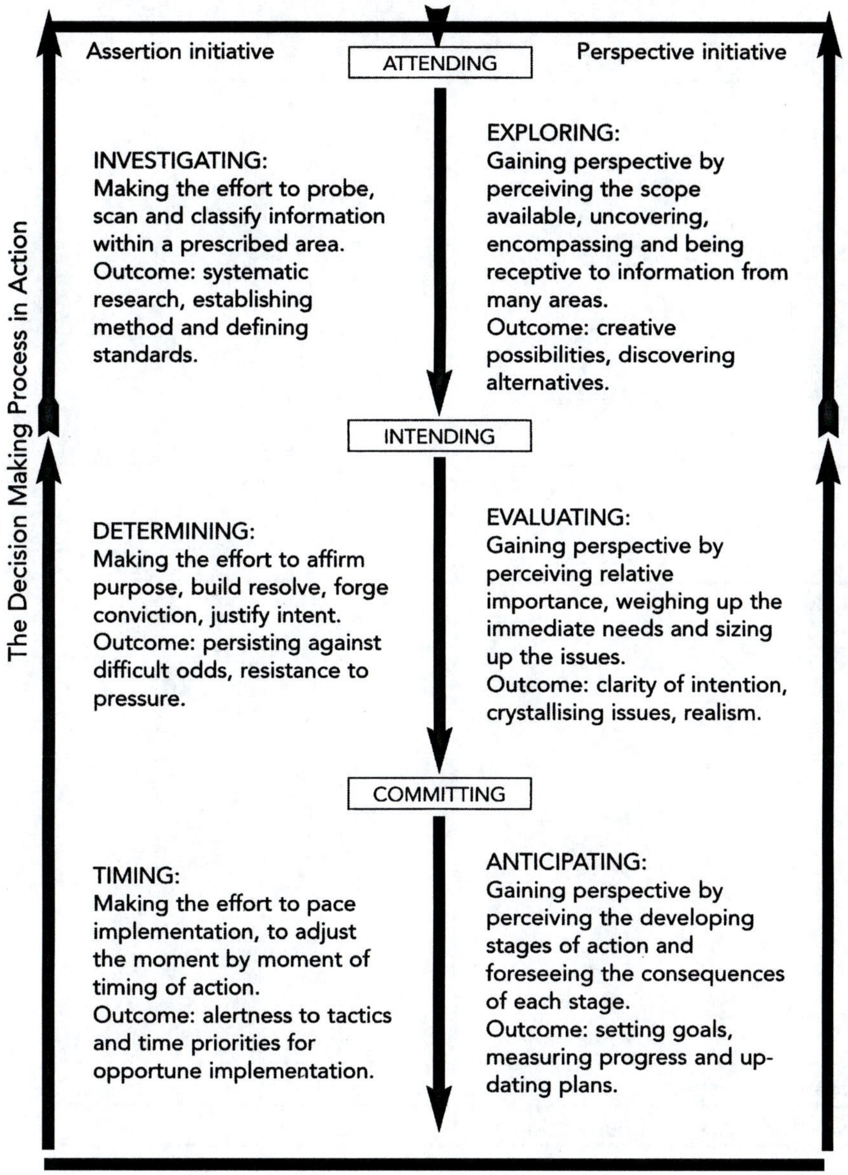

The Decision Making Process in Action

Assertion initiative — ATTENDING — Perspective initiative

INVESTIGATING:
Making the effort to probe, scan and classify information within a prescribed area. Outcome: systematic research, establishing method and defining standards.

EXPLORING:
Gaining perspective by perceiving the scope available, uncovering, encompassing and being receptive to information from many areas. Outcome: creative possibilities, discovering alternatives.

INTENDING

DETERMINING:
Making the effort to affirm purpose, build resolve, forge conviction, justify intent. Outcome: persisting against difficult odds, resistance to pressure.

EVALUATING:
Gaining perspective by perceiving relative importance, weighing up the immediate needs and sizing up the issues. Outcome: clarity of intention, crystallising issues, realism.

COMMITTING

TIMING:
Making the effort to pace implementation, to adjust the moment by moment of timing of action. Outcome: alertness to tactics and time priorities for opportune implementation.

ANTICIPATING:
Gaining perspective by perceiving the developing stages of action and foreseeing the consequences of each stage. Outcome: setting goals, measuring progress and up-dating plans.

Fig. 19

A conjecture based on analysis of movement impression RUDOLF LABAN		% of total activity	Extent of interaction activity		
Assertion	Perspective			Sharing	Private
Investigating		15	Communicating	75%	45%
ATTENTION	Exploring	26			
Determining		3	Presenting	60%	30%
INTENTION	Evaluating	7			
Timing		25	Operating	90%	15%
COMMITMENT	Anticipating	24			
Assertion/Perspective ratio		43/57			
Dynamism on a ten-point scale		9			

Fig. 20. Profile of Rudolf Laban prepared by Warren Lamb

Laban's preference for sharing his initiatives to such an extent, with little need for privacy, also has significance with regard to relative dependence/independence. Sharing [together with other things] is essential for charisma; a loner or recluse cannot be charismatic. But it also makes a person dependent upon others, which itself usually has the effect of inviting support. Loners do not invite support and they try to solve problems independently. Laban is neither motivated to confront problems nor to fight lone battles. He wants almost always to have people around him.

All I have tried to offer in this brief conjecture are some possible clues to what might have motivated Laban to act the way he did. They are offered to try and give understanding of the man from a different angle.

I mentioned earlier that circumstances often force us to act contrary to our pattern of preference. For example, a person may be desperate not to lose his job and therefore conforms to a situation with which he disagrees and accepts an environment he hates. This is an extreme example of the sort of compromise all of us are making all the time. This sort of compromise was probably more absent from Laban's behaviour than is the case with the great majority of people. He followed his pattern of preference, probably, almost completely and retired ill when circumstances frustrated him. Had he been born fifty years later the same pattern of initiatives could have led to a similar creative output in more supportive conditions.

APPENDIX II

THE LABAN LAWRENCE TEST FOR SELECTION AND PLACING OF MANAGEMENT STAFF AND NON MANUAL WORKERS

The following are extracts from two presentations to a client company made by Warren Lamb in 1951 when he was with Paton Lawrence & Co.

Example A is of a "Foreman" carrying responsibilities which in some companies might give him the title of Production Manager. He had been doing the job to the satisfaction of his management for a number of years but recently his behaviour had caused them serious concern. The Laban Lawrence Test was commissioned in order to explain his behaviour and to recommend means for overcoming his difficulties.

Example B is of a short-listed candidate for a new appointment of "Work Study Technician".

In each case the specification relates to the job as it existed in the company concerned.

Specification One
A. FOREMAN

1. Identifying himself with the specified job and not allowing outside considerations to interfere with the performance of his duties.
2. Reviewing a work situation objectively to facilitate balanced judgement.
3. Adjusting and transferring concentration freely to varying demands.
4. Organising the work going through; allotting men and machines so as to make the best use of the resources available.
5. Decisiveness in the day-to-day work where no fixed standards are laid down.
6. Interpreting the firm's policy so far as it affects own department.
7. Realising the precise nature of the job so as to be quite clear of the limits within which he has responsibility.
8. Showing confidence in the service.
9. Translating instructions into action avoiding any distortion.
10. Supervising all work carried out by members of department.
11. Enlisting the workers' support and promoting team work.

12. Presenting self confidently and clearly.
13. Giving general instructions and, where appropriate, individual guidance.
14. Dealing sensitively with people.
15. Incurring respect of individuals in a manner which provides for smooth maintaining of discipline.

Specification Two

B. WORK STUDY TECHNICIAN

1. Observing and recording accurately details of operations and the methods employed.
2. Analysing his observations in detail – finding the crucial element.
3. Recognising the place Work Study can fill in the organisation.
4. Coordinating and cooperating with management and supervisors on all aspects of Work Study.
5. Carrying out interviews; exercising tact and facility of expression.
6. Seeking information over broad range of firm's activities.
7. Defining work relationships; discriminating between job functions.
8. Devising and specifying new methods of operation, administration and management.
9. Appreciating others' point of view; maintaining objectivity.
10. Presenting a case for reorganisation to management; clarity in formulating recommendations.
11. Preparing a comprehensive scheme of reorganisation.
12. Introducing new techniques; finding means for the introduction of new ideas.
13. Adhering to terms of reference in carrying out investigations.
14. Showing initiative where appropriate in seeking out information and making recommendations.
15. Recognising at all stages the relevance of the firm's policy; adapting own approach according to circumstances.
16. Reconciling deviations from a plan; preserving the structure of short or long term planning.
17. Training others in the implementation of a plan.
18. Responding to guidance and training from own superior.

Lamb sat in at a normal interview of each of these people and recorded his observations. After submitting his reports he met their Board to discuss them in the light of information regarding past experience, background and technical qualifications of those tested. He had not previously known these facts. Each report comprised an apportionment of the items of the job specification between:

"CAPACITIES which can be immediately utilised in the carrying out of the job.
"LATENT which can be developed by training and practice to become a capacity.
"INERT which need supervision, provision of specialist advice or delegation of duties."

These, given numerically, are then qualified with longer explanations of their meaning in terms of performance, their Aptitudes. For example:

A. FOREMAN
He is decisive about what action should be taken but almost fearful to reveal it. He employs a craftsman-like use of the senses and registers reactions sensitively. His sensitivity is of this nature and is exceptionally objective. It would help him to show more sensitivity rather than less – he should, for example, not hesitate to comment or take action on his sensing of the mood of the situation.

B. WORK STUDY TECHNICIAN
He possesses a distinct operational skill, is good at organising his task and carrying it through. He has a good sense of sequence but not of time limits; that is he can organise well in terms of a process but not so as to adhere to prescribed schedules. He can clearly mark out stages; is calculating of results and very conscious of his target. He aims fervently to earn personal respect.

Notes on the Inert capacities qualify the inertia shown with regard to certain areas of the job specification, for example:

A. [In relation to item 11 on Specification] Although he promotes action he cannot compose it so as to enlist support from others.
B. [In relation to item 3] Whatever he may know about the place of Work Study he will never be clear in his attitude of the limits to which he is working.

The part of the report dealing with Latent capacities gives advice as to their development with an explanation of why these aspects may not previously have been developed, for example:

A. FOREMAN

If there is one predominant feature which is responsible for his difficulties it may well be his aptitude for promoting some demonstrable action or reaction in others.

Whilst this is often of positive advantage it also obtrudes and to some extent displaces other efforts. It would not apply in the exercise of supervision [see capacity 10] but it does upset his capacity [see Latent 4] for all aspects of organisation in which he has to communicate with the men. Some of his attempts at "organising the work going through" must have quite irrational and unexpected results. If he can be made aware of the present position it should not be difficult for him to discipline his effort in a way which will allow him to exercise a more straightforward organisatory capacity, harnessing more fully his "craftsman-like sensitivity" [see Aptitudes].

In the case of A there was a deputy whose Laban Lawrence Test reported him to be a good organiser. In the course of treatment A revealed some resentment of his deputy's capacity in this respect, being aware of his own difficulties, and was not making use of the deputy as he should. He was later both able to improve his own capacity and make some more use of his deputy.

B. WORK STUDY TECHNICIAN

He can best be trained by a process of conditioning by breaking up the subject matter into brief stages showing tangible results. The conditioning process means that he should be within the environment within which he is to work under some constant stress – there should be nothing remote. The briefer it is possible to make the stages of learning the better. This applies to the carrying out of interviews, a situation in which he will happily indulge, immersing himself in the process of it, but he will be likely to fail in fulfilling some necessary requirement such as exercising tact, consideration of which he will feel is interrupting his "operational skill...at organising his task and carrying it through". He can be trained out of this indulgence, with regard to all the Latent capacities, in the manner indicated above. For example, he should break down the requirements of interviewing technique and organise each occasion in great detail.

NB If B. is appointed, his immediate chief should be a man whose Laban Lawrence Test reported that he had an aptitude for "going into too much detail". It is suggested that this man could give B. just the development he needs.

After the follow-up meetings an "Appreciation" of each situation was written.

A. FOREMAN
[In this case the Appreciation followed a course of training based on the report]
He is now aware of the greater intensity needed for certain acts of adjustment and how he can bring it about.

B. WORK STUDY TECHNICIAN
[Given in question and answer form]
Can he gain the confidence of work people?
He can establish that he is acceptable [*reference is made to the paragraph of Aptitudes from which this is deduced*] but not constructively build up confidence if left to his own resources [*further reference*].

A course of training or treatment given in the case of A. consisted of making the individual aware of the analysis from which the report was deduced and how he must adjust so as to develop Latent capacities and overcome limitations. It has a special application whenever the limitations are severe or a person is under stress.

APPENDIX III

APTITUDE ASSESSMENT FOR A MARKETING DIRECTOR

Extracts from an aptitude assessment presented by Warren Lamb in 1963

I Introduction

The four short-listed candidates are matched in this report against an aptitude specification specially drawn up for the job. An important aspect is that the man appointed will be immediately invited onto the Board and may later have the opportunity to succeed to the Managing Directorship. Potentiality for this is a requirement.

The specification is given in full in Section II, and a comparative matching is given in III. Section IV gives a summary for each candidate and this should explain the apportionment of the items of the specification shown in III. Finally, Section V offers a Recommendation.

The aim is to present enough information on aptitude which, when allied with information on skill and experience, will facilitate a decision. In the case of the candidate appointed the Summary can, if desired, be extended and advice on induction and development included.

II Aptitude Specification

1. Familiarising himself quickly with the present position; finding out the facts on which to recommend a revised marketing policy.
2. Appreciating trends in the trade and exploring all outlets for opportunities which the Company can exploit commercially with the limited resources available.
3. Discriminating objectively and ruthlessly in his selection or rejection of possibilities to be followed up.
4. Persevering in the consistent application of Marketing policy; not allowing any distracting influences.
5. Devising methods for implementation of policy; courage and conviction in replacing present procedures where justified.
6. Having ideas for sales promotion, both on the products themselves and methods of selling; original, creative thinking.
7. Carrying out market research; planning campaigns; conducting test-marketing programmes; utilising specialist and agency services where appropriate.

8. Negotiating contracts and special agreements so as to cater for long term interests.
9. Obtaining and communicating a grasp of the Company's activities as a whole so as to establish authority in all departments.
10. Superintending work of subordinates and liaison with departmental heads in a manner which generates enthusiasm.
11. Establishing clear general management priorities and allocating resources accordingly.
12. Taking initiative in policy formation and seeing that policy is translated into action through delegation of work.
13. Adapting to close informal association with colleagues in work discussion and identifying himself with top level interests.
14. Putting emphasis on the essentials at any particular time in guiding staff and setting standards.
15. Getting others' co-operation; promoting mutual trust.
16. Taking opportunities to develop own capacity and stature in line with developing Company interests.

III Matching of Candidates Against Aptitude Specification

Items abbreviated from the list given in II

	Mr A	Mr B	Mr C	Mr D
1. FAMILIARISING HIMSELF	C	A	B	B
2. APPRECIATING TRENDS	A	A	C	A
3. DISCRIMINATING	A	A	B	A
4. PERSEVERING	B	A	C	B
5. DEVISING METHODS	A	B	A	C
6. IDEAS	C	B	A	C
7. MARKET RESEARCH	B	A	A	B
8. NEGOTIATING	A	A	B	A
9. OVERALL AUTHORITY	C	A	C	A
10. SUPERINTENDING	A	C	C	A
11. ESTABLISHING PRIORITIES	A	B	C	A
12. INITIATIVE	B	B	C	A
13. IDENTIFICATION	C	A	B	A

14. GUIDING STAFF	C	A	A	A
15. GETTING COOPERATION	C	B	A	A
16. DEVELOPING OWN STATURE	B	A	C	A

Key:

A   Active [Spontaneous to requirements]

B   Latent [Some tentativeness; showing promise of becoming a response]

C   Inert [Possibility of a spontaneous response has deteriorated and requirement can only be met through conscious control]

IV SUMMARIES

MR A

He has his own private code of conduct and will impose this on a situation rather than seek out a particularly appropriate approach. He is alert but not penetratingly observant. There is little real effort to familiarise himself or identify himself, and such ideas as he has will be more opportunistically imposed than born out of assessment of the Company's needs.

He is strong on his appreciation of general trends, and will always give the impression of knowing his mind. He has intense, tautly expressed convictions, which he will seek to back up through emphasis rather than explanation. This may make him obstinate. He can discriminate only at the cost of underlining a partisan attitude, and his influence will be more to divide a group than unite it. Colleagues would feel his competitiveness and subordinates his arbitrariness.

It needs a strong, well-systematised, status oriented organisation for him to make the most of his positive attitude. Alternatively, he might be used effectively in an agent-like position, as though an outsider offering specialist services.

MR B.

He lacks a natural authoritativeness, often presents himself inadequately, fails to press home an advantage, and in general suffers from bad timing. Despite these deficiencies, matched against the job under review, his only serious handicap is in superintending subordinates, in which he may fail both to generate enthusiasm and to instil discipline.

The lack of authority and presentation makes him work his passage to achieve what others may attempt through flair, with consequent sound long term results. His 'worrying' is just healthy, conscientious hard work – there is no stress element in it. His failure to press home an advantage and bad timing makes him pause before taking initiative and this is related to some difficulty in establishing priorities, but he will develop more facility in these things the more he thinks as a Director as well as a Manager, a distinction which he will make clearly. He is particularly suited to the exercise of an overall responsibility – he is not a specialist – and at the same time he is able to differentiate very clearly between different functions.

His positive aptitude derives mainly from an exceptional facility for penetrating to the essentials of a problem or situation and persevering to a conclusion.

It will help him to work in close contact with colleagues, where free and informal interplay of ideas is encouraged, and where he can test out on others the effect of his proposals in their formative stage.

MR C

He has style, method, a teacher-like facility for giving guidance, and a tortured creativeness. These are linked in a sort of masochistic need he has for prolonging the agony of a decision. He will expatiate on a task when others will just go ahead and do it. He is essentially an adviser. As an executive director his didacticism would drive to distraction.

He lacks self-reliance and cannot help but become to some extent subservient to the will of his superiors. This makes him very demanding of colleagues' time and magnanimity. Much of his effort is in satisfaction of a personal need rather than orientated towards an objectively set target. He has aims, not targets; declared principles in place of decisive action; and appeal instead of attack.

He might make a good management trainer.

MR D

He has a power complex and will usurp power if he has half the chance. He is therefore a man of whom to beware. On the other hand he offers an exceptionally resolute, convinced, determined approach to his job which will carry many colleagues and subordinates with him, and achieve results through the sheer force of leadership.

His big failing is that he is liable to become convinced on inadequate premises, and he does not probe enough to come up with anything original. There is a danger of his becoming completely unstuck. Right or wrong, he never does anything by halves.

He uses other people dispassionately yet sensitively and in a well-planned and organised way. He exploits his leadership through good tactical planning. He is a resourceful operator.

He would monopolise as Marketing Manager – no-one else would get a chance to contribute other than at his behest. And as Managing Director he would create very much a one man show.

V RECOMMENDATIONS

1. Mr A should be eliminated on the grounds that his specialist type of marketing is too limited to meet the requirements.

2. Mr C must be eliminated as someone who would give more trouble than service.

3. Mr B and Mr D are suitable in that both have the aptitude to achieve results in the conditions under review.

4. In making a choice between these two it boils down to the following contrast:
   A] Inviting to join a team [Mr B]
   B] Handing over [Mr D]

   Whilst D may have its attractions it is probably impracticable and has its dangers, particularly if the potential Managing Directorship is taken into account. This leaves Mr B, whose greater humility may prove more acceptable and, in the long run, more fruitful. He can positively be recommended.

BIBLIOGRAPHY

An Interview with Warren Lamb, Susan M. Lovell, American Journal of Dance Therapy, Vol. 15, Spring/Summer 1993.

The Laban Lecture from Anna Carlisle, The Laban Guild Movement and Dance Quarterly, Vol. 19, No. 3, Autumn 2000.

A Life for Dance by Rudolf Laban, translated and annotated by Lisa Ullmann. Published Macdonald and Evans, 1965.

Body Code: The Meaning of Movement by Warren Lamb and Elizabeth Watson, London, Routledge & Kegan Paul, 1979.

Empirical Studies of Posture-Gesture Mergers, Deborah du Nann Winter together with Carla Widell, Gail Truitt, Jane George-Falvy, *Journal of Nonverbal Behaviour*, 1989, Human Sciences Press.

Labanotation or Kinetography Laban [second edition] by Ann Hutchinson, London, OUP, 1970.

Management Behaviour by Warren Lamb and David Turner, London, Gerald Duckworth & Co, 1969.

Man of the Month, 153, Rudolf Laban, interview by Olive Moore, October 1954 for Scope magazine for Industry.

Mountain of Truth Martin Green, University Press of New England, 1986.

Movement Analysis becomes a tool of industry by Warren Lamb, Dance Magazine, January 1952.

Once I had laughter: a tribute to the fortitude of the human spirit, by Hettie Loman, with Kinetography Laban Dance Score by Sally Archbutt. 1990. Croydon Dance Theatre, 1988.

Posture and Gesture by Warren Lamb, London, Gerald Duckworth &Co., 1965.

Rudolf Laban, An Extraordinary Life, by Valerie Preston Dunlop, London, Dance Books, 1998.

The Body Mind Connection in Human Movement Analysis Ed. Susan Loman MA, ADTR with Rose Brandt MA, Antioch, New England Graduate School, Keene, NH, 1992.

The Dartington Hall Archive, Totnes, Devon.

The Kinaesthetic Approach to Piano Technique, by Warren Lamb and Ronald Meachen, London, 1962–63, Ed. Eden Davies. Brechin Books Ltd, London 2003.

The Meaning of Movement, Development and Clinical Perspectives of the Kestenberg Movement Profile, Amighi, Loman, Lewis and Sossin, Gordon and Breach for Overseas Publishers Association, N.V., 1999.

The National Resource Centre for Dance, University of Surrey, Guildford.

The Theory and Management Applications of Action Profiling®, A Technique for Identifying Individual Movement Patterns, an MSc thesis by Tim Lamb, Imperial College of Science and Technology, London 1985.

Top Team Planning, by Pamela Ramsden, London, Cassell/Associated Business Programmes Ltd, 1973.

Validation of Action Profiling, a paper by Tim Lamb.